How to Build and Manage an

Environmental Law Practice

by Stuart L. Somach

SECTION OF ENVIRONMENT, ENERGY, AND RESOURCES
LAW PRACTICE MANAGEMENT SECTION

Cover design by Gail Patejunas.

Nothing contained in this book is to be considered as the rendering of legal advice for specific cases, and readers are responsible for obtaining such advice from their own legal counsel. This book and any forms and agreements herein are intended for educational and informational purposes only.

The products and services mentioned in this publication are under or may be under trademark or service mark protection. Product and service names and terms are used throughout only in an editorial fashion, to the benefit of the product manufacturer or service provider, with no intention of infringement. Use of a product or service name or term in this publication should not be regarded as affecting the validity of any trademark or service mark.

The American Bar Association offers educational programs for lawyers in practice. Books and other materials are published in furtherance of these programs. Authors and editors of publications may express their own legal interpretations and opinions, which are not necessarily those of either the American Bar Association; the Section of Environment, Energy, and Resources; or the Law Practice Management Section unless adopted pursuant to the bylaws of the Association. The opinions expressed do not reflect in any way a position of the Sections or the American Bar Association.

© 2000 American Bar Association. All rights reserved.
Printed in the United States of America.

04 03 02 01 00   5 4 3 2 1

Somach, Stuart L.
    How to build and manage an environmental law practice / Stuart L. Somach.
        p. cm.
    Includes index.
    ISBN 1-57073-732-0
    1. Practice of law–United States. 2. Environmental law–United States.
    I. Title.

KF300.S66 1999
344.73'046–dc21   99-46842
                                                                            CIP

Discounts are available for books ordered in bulk. Special consideration is given to state bars, CLE programs, and other bar-related organizations. Inquire at Book Publishing, American Bar Association, 750 N. Lake Shore Drive, Chicago, Illinois 60611.

Contents

CHAPTER 11
Location of Your Practice   119

CHAPTER 12
A Last Word   125

About the Author

STUART L. SOMACH is a founding shareholder with the Sacramento law firm of De Cuir & Somach. He is a former Honors Program Attorney, United States Department of the Interior. He also served as an Assistant U.S. Attorney and Senior Trial Attorney, U.S. Department of Justice. Mr. Somach entered private practice in 1984. His practice includes the representation of both public entities and private clients throughout the Western United States in land use and development matters involving wetlands, wildlife and natural resources regulations, water availability, and general environmental matters. He specializes in water rights and water quality law, natural resource and general environmental law, as well as litigation in federal and state courts. Mr. Somach has taught water rights, natural resources, and environmental courses, and is an Adjunct Professor of Law at the University of the Pacific McGeorge School of Law. Mr. Somach has authored numerous law review and other articles in the area of environmental law. He is a past Chairman of the American Bar Association's Committee on Water Resources Law, and Attorney-Delegate to the Ninth Circuit Judicial Conference. Prior to entering law school, Mr. Somach taught junior high school. He lives in Sacramento, California, with his wife Christine, has two grown children, and spends a great deal of his free time reading and running.

The publications of the Section of Environment, Energy, and Resources and the Law Practice Management Section have a commitment to quality. Our authors and editors are outstanding professionals and active practitioners in their fields. In addition, prior to publication, the contents of all of our books are rigorously reviewed by the Section's Book Publications Committee and outside experts to ensure the highest quality product and presentation.

Acknowledgments

Everything contained in this book was gleaned through my observation of others. To the extent that I have had the opportunity to try most of it myself and have had success at it is, to a large degree, a testament to those from whom I have learned. I have, indeed, had good teachers.

I thank the ABA Section of Environment, Energy, and Resources, from which I have derived a lot, for asking me to undertake this effort, including Kathleen Marion Carr, who first contacted me about the project. As I grappled with the organization and then the writing of the manuscript, I chose to rely upon what I knew, with the thought that over time, if there was interest, I could refine the contents with the experiences and suggestions of others. As a consequence, it is not possible to thank all of those who assisted. However, the individual and collective wisdom of others permeates this volume.

My law firm, De Cuir & Somach, and its associates, staff, and shareholders have always been where they should be, and have provided me with a safe and secure "home" where I could always find the professional support essential to a successful practice. Dennis De Cuir, who has patiently explained to me (often) the right way to manage a law firm, deserves a lot of the credit for making me understand the more subtle points of client relations as well as the "business" part of the practice of law. My partners, including

Paul Simmons and Sandra Dunn, have always been supportive, and for that I owe them more than just a simple thank you.

Elizabeth Spence helped me a great deal with the chapter focusing on litigating away from home. Not only did she provide material for the chapter, but she lived through the experience (more than once) with me. Susan Bentley, who has assisted me in the practice of law almost since the first day I entered private practice, not only typed the manuscript but also offered her critical editorial eye to the effort.

I also want to thank Rick Paszkiet at ABA Publishing who babysat me through the entire time that I labored over the development of the manuscript. His patience, suggestions, and encouragement were appreciated, as were the critical comments of the editorial review panel.

I want to thank my parents for, among other things, instilling in me an inescapable sense of responsibility toward those who rely upon me. That and the hard work they demonstrated in their own endeavors provided me with an understanding of the most critical elements of success.

There are my children, Rebecca and Cory, who, no matter how caught up I became with the practice of law, always were there, providing me with love and a perspective that prevented me from taking anything but them too seriously.

Finally, there is my wife, Christine, my partner in everything and the one person who has made success in the practice of law and in life available to me. There is simply no way that I could have learned what I have learned or achieved what I have achieved without her; nor would I have wanted to.

The Nature of an Environmental Law Practice

1

THERE ARE ANY NUMBER OF mechanical or process-related steps that you can and, to a certain degree, must undertake in order to establish a successful environmental law practice. This book discusses these things and encourages their use. Nonetheless, I believe that it is important to note at the outset that the pure employment of mechanical or process-oriented steps alone will not and cannot ensure success. The foundation of success in building and maintaining an environmental law practice or, indeed, any law practice, is much more basic and deals with how you view and relate to the practice of law. Unless, at a very early stage, this underlying concept is explored with a firm understanding of its significance, no mere mechanical or process-related steps are likely to be helpful. Because I firmly believe this and because I know that little focus is ever given to this perspective, I start from this concept.

I cannot begin to remember all of the people with whom I have talked who wanted to "get into the law so that they could protect the environment." They talk about the importance of the environment. They talk about all that they can do to protect the environment. However, rarely, if ever, do they say that they want to be lawyers; nor do I hear them focus on, or even recognize, the economic reality of attempting to pursue environmental law as a career. Perhaps this situation exists with other careers or within other areas of the law, but in my view, not understanding that entering a career in environmental law means that you must become, act, and think like a lawyer—and that there is an economic component to the practice of environmental law like there is in any other business—is a serious problem that dooms people to a job that they may not like or saddles them with expectations that cannot be met. Focusing, at least for a minute, on these real-world concerns can provide a grounding to allow you to pursue a career in environmental law with realistic expectations.

I remember pondering in law school the type of law that I might want to practice. I had spent a few years in graduate school after college and about five years teaching junior-high school before I went to law school. I had a young family to be concerned about and I was focused on succeeding in law school in order to facilitate my success as a lawyer. As a junior-high school teacher I had lived and worked with an idealism that ended up being not as entirely satisfying as I had hoped and left me more than a little bit short at the end of each month when I tried to pay my bills. The "real world" had forced an economic reality on me that, in some respects, I would have preferred avoiding. As a consequence, as a law student, I assumed that a more traditional civil-business practice was what I wanted because, among other things, it appeared to be a safe and stable legal career path.

My study partner at the time had other ideas. He was right out of college and what he wanted was to protect the environment. A course in environmental law had just been started at the law school and the obvious focus of his intentions was on enrolling in that course and forging ahead with a career in environmental law.

At the time I was about as environmentally minded as you could get. I had taught various environmental and "nature" related courses and had been the faculty sponsor of the seventh- and eighth-grade Backpacking Club. However, I thought the idea of practicing environmental law a bit odd. I told him: "You cannot make money practicing environmental law. I am not interested."

I did not take that environmental law class. My view of environmental law involved the idealistic notion of "protecting the environment" fostered by the popular images of environmentalists facing down those who would cut down the rain forests or kill helpless animals. It did not at all involve the legal concepts that I was learning about in law school; nor did it seem to me to relate to the things that lawyers, other than public-interest lawyers, did to make a living. While I wish it might be otherwise, this perception (or perhaps misperception) of the law that I held then was not then and is not now unique. Although today most law students have a bit broader context and understanding of the field of environmental law and are aware that you can make a living in the practice of environmental law, they almost all also carry with them some variation of this basic misperception about what an environmental lawyer does. New lawyers interviewing for a job with my firm or who contact me about jobs in environmental law also often carry with them this perception.

In one sense this perception of what environmental law is remains a significant problem. It was only through circumstances that I could not even imagine in law school that I ended up an environmental lawyer. The point is, however, that environmental law is much more than this popular perception. The practice of the law, in fact, involves and requires a broad understanding of the rich textures of the law—it does not just focus on the environment. And it most certainly does relate to the real-world consideration that lawyers need to deal with in order to make a living.

In addition, establishing an environmental law practice today requires understanding that the field of environmental law is not what it was in the 1960s or in the 1970s when I began to practice. As a consequence, while still a vibrant area of the law, the opportunities that exist now are different from what they once were.

An environmental law practice is, in its most fundamental aspect, no different than any other area of legal practice. This point I believe to be crucial. The good environmental lawyer must first be a good lawyer. The key to a successful environmental law practice, therefore, is no different than any other successful law practice. The successful environmental lawyer must be a good lawyer, enjoy the practice of law, and also enjoy working with clients.

While these fundamental statements may seem obvious, as a practical matter, this basic understanding of what it takes to have a successful environmental law practice is often lost. In particular, in the practice of environmental law, you tend to focus on the environmental aspect of being an environmental lawyer and to de-emphasize the lawyer part. This tendency probably derives from two aspects unique to this area of the law.

First, the environment and environmental law involve issues of great societal importance that, at times, rise to the fervor of a moral cause or crusade. Indeed, the environment and the need to protect it have resulted, for example, in worldwide events such as Earth Day and the creation of political "green" parties. Environmental law is policy intensive. It is a dynamic area of the law that is driven by an underlying ethic that revolves around core concerns associated with events and situations that directly affect everyone. It can be very political in its nature.

This basic aspect of this area of the law needs to be understood and accounted for in the establishment of a successful environmental law practice. While lawyers can and do play a large role in the moral and political dialog that revolves around this area of the law, the successful environmental lawyer must, at the outset of practice, decide how he or she wishes to position the practice. Will the practice be "political," in the nature of a lobbying practice? Will it advocate for one side or the other (assuming, of course, that the complex issues can be clearly divided into "sides")? Or will the practice focus not on the broader societal issues at play but rather on the representation of clients with real and sometimes mundane problems?

Successful practices can be built to emphasize any of these focuses, but probably not to deal with all of them.

The second broad aspect of this area of the law to consider is the recognition that the law is but an element of the much larger world of environmental problem-solving and environmental concerns. This larger world involves an amazingly diverse array of complex and technical issues. As a consequence, other professional disciplines have a direct stake and role in the development and implementation of policy and, in turn, the law.

This results in a view that the good environmental lawyer is one who has knowledge of chemistry, biology, engineering, toxicology, or any of the almost countless other disciplines that may be needed or involved in addressing any given environmental problem or issue; and that a sound and broad grounding in the law is of secondary importance, which, if lacking, can be overcome by having a good technical foundation.

This view is reinforced because relevant rules, regulations, and even certain statutory procedures and substantive provisions are themselves technical in nature, and having technical knowledge is essential to fully understanding the law and, in turn, providing appropriate representation. Nevertheless, the practice of environmental law is still the practice of the law.

There are no shortcuts. A successful environmental law practice is grounded upon the same foundations as any other successful law practice. Being expert in the drafting of contracts; understanding real property concepts or other transactional lawyering skills; applying the elements of a tort claim to an environmental setting; being able to utilize or hurdle procedural aspects of a challenge to a rule or regulation and, in this context and in its broader application, an understanding of administrative law principles; being able to expertly litigate, regardless of the nature of the environmental cause of action; and enjoying these practice areas are what is at the core of a successful environmental law practice. The technical aspects of toxicology, biology, or other professional fields that interact with the practice of environmental law (and even the broader societal issues that are implicated) are merely the spice that adds the unique flavor to this area of practice.

There is a strongly held view, which I share, that in hiring lawyers to work in an environmental law firm, what is important is not to find someone who has technical knowledge or even a pre-existing disposition or interest in environmental law, but rather to focus on finding a good lawyer. You can always teach smart, creative lawyers about the nonlegal, technical aspects of environmental law. It is infinitely more difficult (and sometimes not possible) to teach someone to become a good lawyer.

Assuming this foundation, the key to success is the same as what should make any law practice successful. The lawyer must enjoy the practice. It does not matter what techniques are used to market the practice, what equipment is purchased or what legal materials are available; if you do not enjoy the practice of law, and ultimately the practice of environmental law, the goal of a truly successful law practice will always elude you.

In this context, you cannot enjoy the practice of law, and thus build and maintain a successful environmental law practice, unless you enjoy working with your clients. Again, this seems obvious. However, in the area of environmental law there tends to be a baffling focus on the broader aspects of the environment with lawyers often more interested in the issues than in the people who may be most directly affected. You may be a very talented lawyer who revels in the intellectual and "global" issues associated with the environment and environmental law. However, a practice that focuses on the issues and forgets that it is important to know, enjoy, and care for clients, is a practice that can only have limited, if any, lasting success.

The foundational keys to a successful environmental law practice are simply stated and seemingly obvious. To be a successful environmental lawyer, you must be a good lawyer, enjoy the practice of law, and enjoy working with clients. Understanding these points and developing what is necessary to attain them ought to allow you to focus on the more mechanical steps that you can utilize in order to develop a successful environmental law practice.

Selecting an Environmental Specialty or Specialties

2

EARLIER I NOTED THAT you needed to decide how you wanted to position yourself in the practice of environmental law. I pointed out that the practice could be "political" in the nature of lobbying; it could be a practice that advocated a certain position in the larger environmental debate and dialog that exists; or it could focus on more traditional concepts of client representation. A related matter of equal importance is a decision about what kind of environmental law you want to practice: the specific technical discipline or disciplines on which you wish to focus.

The term "environmental law" encompasses a great deal. Indeed, it would be difficult, if not impossible, to find a definition of environmental law that would be able to cover all of the possible practice areas that are conceivably involved. The purpose of this book is not to deal substantively with any aspect of environmental law, but rather to provide insight into those things that can be done to enhance the opportunity for success in the practice of environmental law. A primary step is to understand the breadth of what is considered "environmental law"

7

and to assist you in determining the areas of this body of law on which you intend to focus. Because practice within the various areas of environmental law may be quite different, what is necessary to be successful in one area may not lend itself to success in another area. Moreover, each specialty area carries with it very different expectations with respect to the nature of the practice involved.

While the need to focus is a critical element of the environmental law practice, it is important to warn you about the danger of being too focused. In some respects the understanding of what environmental law is all about boils down to the fact that everything in the environment is, in one manner or another, connected to everything else. There is an inherent danger in attempting to overly compartmentalize areas of environmental law. The complete and successful representation of clients may well involve knowledge, competence, and skill in a number of areas of environmental law. At a minimum, it will require an ability to identify these areas so that a client may be referred to other practitioners if your own practice does not extend to all of the areas of concern. Defining limits is as much an aspect of a successful law practice as is determining the focus of the practice.

It is also important to understand the historic context in which a practice is to be developed. Environmental law today is not the same as it was thirty years ago or even ten years ago.

Environmental law is not new. The general question of environmental protection has existed for a very long time. The history of the law is replete with examples of attempts to address the concerns associated with population growth, development, and resource exploitation. In the United States, this law first developed as a means to avoid conflicts associated with competing resource use. Protection of the environment per se was not a focus of the law, with the exception of early preservation efforts in the East. Pure environmentalism was not generally embraced by the law. That field was occupied by visionaries who acted on a broader stage.

Because environmental issues presented themselves to the law as a matter of conflict—for example, where dust or smoke from an industrial plant adversely affected a neighbor's use of property, or where a diversion of water affected the ability of others to generate power through a water wheel—environmental law focused on conflict resolution, with the protection of the environment not really at issue. Early environmental cases focused on tort and nuisance theories more than anything else.

The real precursor to modern environmental law did not take shape until environmental problems could not be dealt with solely as a matter of resolving conflicts between a limited number of people. Broader environmental concerns that affected much larger populations and that were associated with polluted air and water led in the late 1940s to federal legislation. These statutes, for the most part, did not result in an extensive development of a body of environmental law because most of the significant potential protections were left to the states. The states, being much closer to the issues—including the economic consequences of the potential solutions to environmental problems—did little, if anything, meaningful to address identified problems, and again, common law theories of conflict resolution predominated.

In the 1960s, there was broader general focus on social issues, coupled with increasing problems associated with air pollution, water pollution, and the consequences of the almost unregulated use of insecticides, herbicides, and other toxic substances. People became concerned about clear-cutting in our national forests, the preservation of our wild land and waters, animal and plant species extinction, and the need for what is now commonly referred to as biodiversity. This is when real, broadly based development in the area of environmental law emerged.

At the federal level, Congress enacted a series of significant statutory provisions covering a wide range of environmental topics. First, Congress enacted the National Environmental Policy Act (NEPA), a statutory provision that required agencies of the United States to focus on the environmental consequences of their actions and programs. NEPA's requirement that major federal actions that might have a significant adverse impact on the human environment be the subject of an environmental impact statement (EIS) has had significant, long-lasting impact in almost all aspects of federal decision making.

After the enactment of NEPA, Congress followed with amendments to the Clean Air Act (CAA) and Clean Water Act (CWA) that put teeth in those old statutes and that no longer deferred to the states for implementation and enforcement. In addition, Congress enacted statutes like the Resource Conservation and Recovery Act (RCRA) and Comprehensive Environmental Response, Compensation, and Liability Act (CERCLA) to fill gaps in the law that focused on problems associated with toxic chemicals and their use. Other similar statutes, focused on specific identified concerns, were also enacted. In addition, the Environmental Protection Agency (EPA) was created along with the Council on Environmental Quality (CEQ). For the first time, there were agencies of the federal government whose main mission was the protection of the environment.

A great deal of environmental legislation, or regulation, was also enacted on the resources side of the environmental question. The federal Endangered Species Act (ESA) was enacted to control federal and nonfederal actions that might affect endangered or threatened animal or plant species. How the Forest Service and Bureau of Land Management managed federal lands was significantly modified with the enactment of the National Forest Management Act of 1976 (NFMA), the Multiple User-Sustained Yield Act (MUSY) and the Federal Land Policy Management Act (FLPMA). The enactment of the federal Wilderness Act and the federal Wild and Scenic Rivers Act set aside and protected expanses of land and water from further development. Numerous other statutes and regulations were enacted to refocus use of federal land and water away from development or single use and toward conservation and preservation or multiple uses. In addition, the federal government and its agencies were subject in almost all of their actions to the broad environmental statutory provisions noted above.

All of these federal actions also had an impact on the states. Most of the federal environmental statutory provisions had provisions allowing the states to implement these laws within the states, assuming that state implementing legislation was "at least as stringent" as what was provided under federal law. Under the federal statutory structure, the EPA would make determinations of the sufficiency of the state provisions and would continue to monitor state actions. Many states also enacted their own NEPA-like provisions; resource preservation at the federal level found a parallel at the state level with the protection of plant and animal species as well as "wild lands" being expanded.

Local government was also involved with the public-health and safety aspects of environmental law, with aspects of the law dealing with clean air or clean water being regulated by counties or cities. In addition, local government was subject to the state NEPA analysis with respect to its actions. Finally, local land-use and zoning laws and decisions shifted greatly to accommodate need for open space and recreation, and, in general, to accommodate the needs of a more environmentally sensitive society.

All of this, at the federal, state, and local levels, was done almost from a dead start in the 1960s, resulting in the extensive maze of statutory environmental provisions that exist as we move into the next century.

Moreover, the statutory provisions, extensive in themselves, were all augmented through the development of volumes of rules and regulations of a highly complex and technical nature. Many of these rules and regulations were contested with the regulated parties challenging their promulgation almost every step of the way. It was in this context that, as it developed, the body of statutory and regulatory environmental law also generated an impressive body of environmental case law, much of it focused on the nuances of administrative law at the federal, state, and local levels.

All of this activity resulted in real progress in dealing with environmental problems. It also generated a lot of legal work. In barely forty years the law developed from infancy to middle age. This development included the creation of new agencies and departments at the federal, state, and local levels, all of which needed to be staffed with administrative, technical, and legal personnel. It also meant the promulgation of rules and regulations to implement these statutory provisions, a process that included extensive technical and legal work coupled with adherence to strict processes mandated by the law.

Once enacted and promulgated, these statutory and regulatory provisions needed to be implemented and enforced both in administrative and judicial forums and, over time, continued to be administered. Additionally, many of these statutory provisions had citizen-suit provisions that allowed private citizens or, more likely, environmental advocacy groups, to sue the relevant state or federal agency in an attempt to force these agencies to do what the law mandated they do, or to attempt themselves to implement or enforce the law when it was thought that federal or state implementation or enforcement was wanting.

All of these federal, state, local, or citizen-related actions, of course, required responsive actions on the part of the regulated community. This responsive action, whether as part of an implementation or enforcement effort or as part of a proactive environmental program implemented to ensure compliance, required armies of technical and legal personnel to assist in negotiating a way through the environmental laws, rules, and regulations that had now been established.

There was, quite simply, more than enough work, legal and otherwise, to go around. The legal market, in these areas, was not only wide open, but it could be quite lucrative.

That situation has, however, changed and the legal market in the area of environmental law is quite different from what it once was. Indeed, this is one of the most sobering areas for lawyers who want to enter environmental law to understand. The notion that environmental law is a new and burgeoning area of the law is simply not accurate.

While young in the pure chronological sense, the amount of energy and focus that have been devoted to this area of the law have aged it beyond its years. As a consequence, the opportunities for a new lawyer within the field of environmental law that existed only ten years ago simply are no longer there.

While I believe that there is always room for good lawyers in any area of the law and opportunities exist to undertake creative and rewarding assignments, the boom years are over. You must have a realistic concept of the market and what is available. That realistic concept must include this new reality of an environmental law practice.

With all this in mind, I have attempted to compile in a very general way all of the possible areas of practice that might be considered to fall under the general umbrella of "environmental law." (I do not claim that this list is exhaustive.) In doing this, I have also attempted to describe the practice skills and the general nature of the practice that is involved.

In addition, I have included an appendix that contains the relevant federal statutory and regulatory provisions that may be implicated in the various areas of environmental law that are listed (see Appendices A and B). As will be dealt with a bit later, it is important to keep in mind that the practice of environmental law is, in the first instance, one of federal law. This does not mean that no state law exists. To the contrary, there is a great deal of law at the state and local levels of which a practitioner must be aware. This is particularly true because federal law encourages the enactment and implementation of state law that is at least as stringent as the federal law. State statutory provisions and regulations vary and, as a consequence, I have not attempted to include them here.

Environmental Regulations for Hazardous Substances

This area of environmental law tends to focus on various federal and state statutes and the rules and regulations that have been promulgated to implement these statutory provisions. In general, this area of the law is most often broken down into and dealt with through physical science categories such as air pollution, water pollution, and toxics. Statutes such as the Federal Insecticide, Fungicide and Rodenticide Act (FIFRA), the Toxics Substances Control Act (TSCA), CERCLA, and RCRA are at the heart of this area of the law, with the Clean Air Act and Clean Water Act also of critical importance.

This area of practice is one that, at various times, involves different practice skills.

Legislative Advocacy

An environmental lawyer may, on behalf of clients with an interest or who will be affected by legislative action in a certain area, contact members of Congress or their staff about the nature and extent of necessary legislation. In this context, environmental lawyers both lobby, advocating an approach or position with respect to the proposed legislation, and provide important technical background and other information for use by the individuals actually drafting the proposed legislation. This type of work can be very time-consuming and involve almost all aspects of the legislative process. In recent years, for example, it has not been unusual for Congress to convene meetings of stakeholders with interests on all sides of an issue to work on and attempt to reach consensus on the best way to proceed. The environmental lawyer can play a crucial role either by directly participating in these discussions and negotiations or in providing counsel to those who are directly involved. This same process, of course, also takes place within the state and local legislative areas.

The Rulemaking Process

Assuming legislation is enacted, practice in this area may turn, at least in part, away from the legislative arena and into the regulatory arena. Lawyers practicing in this area must not only maintain contact with legislators and their staff, but also establish relationships with the regulatory agencies that will be charged with the implementation of these statutory provisions. Implementation work can involve various skills. One aspect involves putting flesh on the statutory bones through the promulgation of rules and regulations. Again, the environmental lawyer will need to become involved as early in this process as possible. Implementing this process through early general discussion of the scope and extent of necessary rules and regulations is crucial. All this can and should take place as a prelude to the formal rulemaking process that must accompany the actual promulgation of rules and regulations.

During the formal rulemaking, the environmental practitioner will need to coordinate the preparation and submission of comments in the manner prescribed for the relevant administrative setting and be able to follow through in all phases of this administrative process. Work in this area may also include the filing of administrative appeals, assuming concern about the regulations that have been promulgated, and possible litigation where considerable concerns exist. Work within this practice area requires continued attention to the rulemaking process since rules and regulations are modified on an almost constant basis. Not viewing rulemaking as an ongoing, rather than a static, process can create problems for the environmental lawyer. You can never assume that the stage is set, but must proceed based upon the knowledge that future modifications in both the statutory, as well as the regulatory, structure can have a direct and sometimes adverse effect upon your client's interests.

Compliance

Once the rules are in place, the environmental lawyer must work to ensure that his or her clients are in compliance with the rules and regulations. This can involve providing advice about operations under the applicable statutes and regulations and, where permits or licenses are involved, assisting the clients in obtaining permits and licenses with which they can live. Obtaining permits and licenses will usually involve some kind of formal hearing process in which evidence is introduced. The environmental lawyer will need to be able to take the lead in this process. Moreover, assuming an unacceptable result, the environmental lawyer will need to be able to appeal and ultimately litigate and, in this context, provide advice on the advisability and utility of challenging regulatory action.

Compliance work in situations with or without a permit may involve providing the type of generalized advice noted earlier. You would hope that this is, in fact, the extent of what compliance work involves. However, compliance work may also involve defending clients in informal inquiries undertaken by administrative agencies or others with respect to alleged violation of statutes, regulations, permits, or licenses, or in more formal enforcement actions.

In a more formal situation, the environmental lawyer may become involved again in a hearing process, introducing evidence and cross-examining or otherwise focusing on specific charges leveled against clients. This type of work is unique in that resolution may involve the crafting of documents that serve as a means of settling disputes in a creative manner that both improves your client's relative operating position, but also meets or even improves upon what was otherwise provided for by regulation, permit, or license to protect the environmental concern.

Formal enforcement work may also include defending clients in civil or criminal enforcement actions within a judicial setting. This type of work is in the nature of more traditional criminal or civil litigation and, in that regard, different from the litigation discussed earlier that focuses on a more limited judicial review of agency decision making. It is, however, more complex than other types of criminal or quasi-criminal litigation because it deals with matters of proof that can be quite complex and technical in nature.

Litigation

Lawyers who practice in this area of the law may also be involved as plaintiffs or defendants in suits attempting to assign liability and responsibility for harm and damages or for a cost recovery under an applicable environmental statute. This type of litigation may involve tort issues (discussed later) but also may involve other more unique problems that require additional skills. For example, because some underlying environmental pollution problems cannot be easily cured or fully addressed in a short period of time, long-term issues must be dealt with. These may include monitoring and remediation, or also involve the sale or purchase of properties. These types of problems may sometimes be solved through indemnification or hold-harmless agreements that transcend what may normally be involved in litigation. Nonetheless, the environmental lawyer must be prepared to deal with these types of problems in a creative way and in a way that involves skills not normally utilized in the litigation context.

In addition, in those situations where agency permitting either is not forthcoming or where permits issued contain terms and conditions not acceptable to clients, environmental lawyers may need to challenge the agency action through litigation. While the reasonable, negotiated resolution of environmental permitting problems is always the best course to follow, sometimes it is just not possible to achieve. In those instances, agency actions may need to be challenged through litigation. This type of litigation generally focuses on administrative agency decision making, but at times can also involve "takings" issues and other related constitutional claims.

Citizen-Suit Litigation

Most of the environmental statutes contain citizen-suit provisions that allow any person the ability to, after appropriate notice, bring suit against alleged violations of statutes, regulations, or permit or license terms and conditions. These provisions of law provide an additional area of litigation unique to the environmental practice.

Over the years the nature of citizen-suit litigation has changed. Initially, most of this type of litigation focused on suits against federal agencies, including the EPA, because of failure on the part of the agency to implement a given environmental law or to promulgate regulations. This litigation involved the plaintiff and government lawyers and also lawyers representing associations or industries with an interest in the general implementation of the law and the nature and extent of the regulations that might be developed for this purpose.

Today, citizen-suit litigation has, more or less, shifted toward compliance issues. A lot of this litigation focuses on individual permits and whether or not they are being adhered to. A prime example of this type of litigation would be citizen suits against publicly owned treatment works (POTWs) related to purported violations of National Pollution Discharge Elimination System (NPDES) permits. NPDES permits require self-monitoring and regulation that are made public. Citizen groups, or lawyers affiliated with these groups, survey the self-monitoring reports and, where they see violations, sue the permittee for penalties under the citizen-suit provisions of the act.

Some of this litigation is, of course, beneficial since it fills a gap in enforcement that may not be adequately covered by regulatory agencies. In all too many situations, however, the suits merely get in the way of regulations, siphoning limited dollars toward what may have been a form of environmental nuisance litigation whose main goal is to perpetuate itself and to generate attorneys' fees for the plaintiff lawyers involved.

Nonetheless, regardless of whether the citizen-suit litigation is properly motivated or not, it has become a part of the environmental law scene, with its own unique attributes. Knowing how to properly represent clients in these types of actions, including the ability to identify the actual nature of the situation, the need to negotiate a reasonable resolution of the dispute, if possible, and the ability to assist clients with the business decisions tied to resolving or litigating a nuisance action, has become an essential part of environmental litigation.

Environmental Consulting

At one point, owning a corner lot in a metropolitan area was a fairly good thing with a lot of economic potential. For example, these were good sites for twenty-four-hour convenience stores. However, most of these sites were also once gas stations, which either once contained or still contain underground storage tanks that had leaked or were still leaking. What the unwary real estate entrepreneur had purchased was an almost open-ended liability. Not only was the new owner at least jointly liable for the cleanup associated with the tank, but if groundwater contamination was implicated, the owner was also responsible for the ongoing monitoring associated with the off-site mitigation of contaminants. Also, the owner could become involved in the search for other potentially responsible parties (PRP) through administrative enforcement or litigation. Now add to the "willing buyer" those who obtained title to these properties through foreclosure or some other indirect manner, and you begin to understand the dimension of the potential problem.

Currently most buyers are aware of these types of problems and auditing properties for environmental problems has become routine, with purchasers factoring in these potential problems as a cost of business and acting accordingly. Nonetheless, this historic example points out a need for environmental review and consideration at almost every stage of doing business. The consequence, both in limitations on proposed actions, as well as the potential significant fines and other financial liability, compel that environmental considerations be factored into the cost of doing routine business. The environmental lawyer needs to be able to fill the necessary role of providing advice in this regard.

Common Law Environmental Law and Toxic Torts

Prior to the late 1960s and the birth of the environmental movement, there did exist a body of common law that was utilized with varying success to address environmental problems. This body of law focused on theories such as nuisance, other intentional or negligent tortious conduct, trespass, and even theories of strict liability. As the environmental movement developed, these common-law theories also developed and became much more complex and sophisticated. This area of practice, often referred to as "toxic torts," includes the need to deal with problems associated with multiple plaintiffs, joint and several liability, complex causation and proof problems, and the development of new types of remedies.

This area of environmental law is, for the most part, an extension of tort law and litigation. The nuance, if any, is that the litigation is extremely technical and complex.

Also, as noted earlier, this type of litigation may be combined with other nontortious theories of liability, including theories that may stem from contract or business relationships such as the sale of contaminated real property, as well as recovery actions associated with certain environmental statutes. Not all of these potential causes of action are best dealt with in the same way. For example, while certainly damages may be a key goal in this type of litigation, cleaning up the property or ensuring that cleanup over time will take place may be of equal importance. As a consequence, proceeding either in bringing these types of actions or defending them requires broad-based and creative lawyering.

It may be, in this regard, that a combination of remedies (some not available in a pure litigation solution) may be appropriate. In this case damages may not be paid, but a defendant or defendants may agree to take full responsibility for cleanup or monitoring.

Indeed, I have even been involved in litigation that was settled through the defendant's purchase of the contaminated property. This required, as a "litigation" skill, the drafting of documents associated with the transfer of extensive real property holdings as part of the stipulated judgment.

Environmental Law—Resources

In addition to the hazardous-substance regulation described earlier, there are also a number of statutory and regulatory provisions that focus on limitations on federal actions and the use of public lands, and also focus on environmental regulation of the use of private lands. These statutory provisions include NEPA, which is a procedural statute that limits federal action, and various specific land-use statutes intended to control the use of both federal as well as private lands. These statutes include the Endangered Species Act and Section 404 of the Clean Water Act. Restrictive state and local laws are most likely also implicated in this area of practice.

Legislative Advocacy

This area of practice is similar to the practice area I described with respect to hazardous substances. In the first instance, it is statutory based with obligations and opportunities to participate in and aid the legislative process. Again, the skills involved here include not only legislative advocacy but also the ability to provide lawmakers with information crucial to their client's interests, which should be considered as part of the legislative process. Stakeholder participation has become an important, even critical, aspect of this type of lawmaking.

Regulatory Practice

Practice in this area of environmental law also includes ongoing, focused interaction with the regulators. The environmental lawyer should establish a working relationship with regulatory staff, and participate in educating them about the world that is being regulated. While regulatory staff may be very knowledgeable from a technical perspective, they may know little, if anything, about the regulated community or the concerns of the environmental community.

As was the case with toxic and hazardous substances, a practitioner in this area of environmental law will need to participate in all phases of formal and informal rulemaking. This includes early contact before rulemaking begins through the participation in preparing comments and, if necessary, appeal and litigation of unsatisfactory results. Again, this area of the law is administrative-law intensive.

Compliance

There is a need to represent clients here with respect to routine compliance. The best example of this may be the potential business endeavor or real estate transaction that implicates an endangered species and runs into the limiting provisions of the Endangered Species Act. Environmental audits need to be undertaken early to avoid unexpected outcomes, and representation of clients in a manner that assists them in avoiding these unexpected pitfalls is an essential part of what environmental lawyers do. Again, how you proceed in this type of representation has the potential of allowing an environmental lawyer to exercise creative skills that might not otherwise come into play. Negotiating with regulatory agencies in order to protect species and also allow a project to be permitted requires a great deal of knowledge of the applicable law, but also the details of the client's intended business undertaking. What is needed here runs the gamut of lawyer skills and, of course, involves a fairly significant degree of technical knowledge as well.

Environmental compliance work, in general, is the area that today holds the greatest prospect for developing and maintaining a viable environmental practice. As the dust has settled, so to speak, this area of environmental law has emerged, in my view, as the most stable, and the area in which clients need the most assistance. Any given situation may give rise to a whole host of compliance issues.

For example, consider the development of rural agricultural lands adjacent to an urbanized area. Initially you would want to conduct an environmental audit to determine if there are any environmental contamination problems associated with past uses. Assuming a clean bill of health in this regard, you would need to next determine if the development of these rural lands is limited or precluded because of limitations associated with the conversion of agricultural lands to urban use. Next the developer will need to proceed through a whole host of local land-use permitting. Some of this is environmental law specific; some has little, if anything, to do with environmental law. In states with mini-NEPAs there may be a requirement for general environmental review and reporting as a condition of local land-use approvals.

In addition to the local issues, there may be specific federal environmental laws that are implicated. If the land has water or wetlands on it, Clean Water Act permitting issues arise. These include obtaining Section 404 permits from the U. S. Army Corps of Engineers and Section 401 water quality certification from the relevant state or local agencies or from the EPA. This permitting might trigger NEPA and would most likely also involve investigations pursuant to the Endangered Species Act (ESA). In addition, assuming these federal issues are implicated, in most states there would also be similar state environmental permitting involved that implicate state departments of game and fish, as well as the state agencies that deal with air and water pollution.

The job of the environmental lawyer is to know what environmental compliance work needs to be undertaken in any given situation and to also know how to proceed with obtaining necessary approvals. As this example demonstrates, in any given situation the environmental and permitting issues may be extensive and diverse. The environmental lawyer must be a key player—in many instances *the* key player—in most aspects of the permitting process.

Litigation

Noncompliance can carry with it significant civil and criminal sanctions. As a consequence, environmental lawyers practicing in this area need to be able to represent clients during investigations and during administrative hearings associated with alleged violations. They must also be able to represent clients in civil and criminal judicial proceedings.

The statutes that dominate this area of the law also include citizen-suit provisions similar to the ones described earlier. These provisions may result in litigation against an agency for an action or a failure to take an action, but in recent years have focused more on individual permittees and their actions. This type of litigation contains an interesting mix of administrative law, in the context of challenged agency decision making, and other types of litigation. Moreover, having one disgruntled party file suit against the agency has the potential of leaving other interested parties out of the litigation. As a consequence, the environmental lawyer must be diligent and be able to understand the ramifications of this type of litigation and make decisions with respect to possible intervention or other means to protect the client's interests.

Finally, there has been and continues to be a great deal of potential for the litigation of "takings" claims in the context of the extensive regulatory scheme that has been put in place under these statutory provisions.

Natural Resources

Natural resource law has traditionally focused on the extraction and use of various resources, including water, minerals (such as hardrock mining, oil, gas, and coal), timber, and the general use of public lands such as the national forests, parks, and other protected areas, as well as open public lands used for grazing. The extraction and use of these resources directly implicates various aspects of both of the environmental regulation areas of practice noted earlier. It is not possible to be a "natural resource lawyer" without also being an "environmental lawyer." The practitioner must integrate the general transactional lawyering skills associated with natural resource law into the environmental context.

Criminal Law

In all of the areas discussed earlier, except with respect to tortious and related conduct, there are, as a parallel to the administrative aspects of the law, also provisions that prescribe criminal sanctions for violations of the law. In many instances these sanctions are quite severe and include monetary penalties, which can be in excess of $25,000 per each day of violation, with the possibility of multiple violations on any one day, in addition to possible jail time.

This area of the law involves general white-collar criminal trial skills. In addition, however, it requires extensive knowledge of substantive provisions of highly complex and technical environmental laws. In this regard, I believe that it is most often appropriate to develop a prosecution or defense team that includes both environmental law specialists as well as criminal law specialists. This area of the environmental legal spectrum has had a history of expansion or contraction depending upon the zeal in environmental criminal enforcement exercised by the U.S. Department of Justice or state attorneys general or local district attorneys. However, in most recent years more prosecutors have become interested in environmental law and more consistent prosecution of these crimes has been undertaken. As a consequence, the defense of environmental crimes has become a much more common and reliable sub-specialty within the criminal practice.

Practice Focus

The descriptions I have provided are a summary and do not contain all of the possible areas of environmental practice, nor do they do justice to the rich fabric of the law as practiced by those in the field. As a caution, not all areas of environmental law provide equal opportunities for the interested potential practitioner.

As noted above, the aging of environmental law has created great shifts in the areas where opportunities exist. Early there was a great deal of work in the areas of advocacy, both legislative and regulatory, and in litigation to force implementation and regulation. Opportunities in these areas are not currently as great as they once were because the legal focus has shifted toward compliance- and permitting-related issues.

As the law has matured, the wide-open opportunities once presented by this "new frontier" of the law have been filled. As a consequence, there is a lot of competition for the available work. This does not mean that success is not possible, but how to achieve it may require a whole host of different skills than what was necessary when the demand for environmental lawyers far exceeded the supply.

Building a Foundation for Your Practice 3

Getting Environmental Experience (Other Than Through Private Practice)

There are, of course, a number of ways you can practice within the area of environmental law. While the focus of this book is on the development of a private practice in environmental law, some discussion of other ways of practicing may, for a variety of reasons, be useful. Practicing outside the private sector is clearly a way you can learn the practical fundamentals of environmental law. Moreover, there are approaches to and views of the law that can only be furthered (or furthered more successfully) through practice outside the private sector. Examples of this are in the prosecution of environmental crimes and work for nonprofit environmental or public-advocacy groups. Finally, in this regard, you might seek to begin an environmental practice outside of the private sector in order to enhance future employment opportunities within the private sector. Experienced government or nonprofit environmental or public-advocacy group lawyers are attractive lateral hires for private firms seeking to either start or expand an environmental law practice.

Government Practice

In some respects, learning through doing and through trial and error may be the best way to perfect skills. The problem, of course, is that no client wants to be the first client on whose behalf a lawyer learns his or her trade, and most law firms have in mind not only client retention but also avoidance of malpractice claims. Consequently, it takes a great deal of time to learn how to become a real lawyer and, by extension, a real environmental lawyer if you begin your practice in the private sector. Learning your trade there tends to be a long, incremental process.

Government lawyering, in contrast, provides a much different type of environment. In this regard, I do not want to be misunderstood. I was a government lawyer, working for both the U.S. Department of the Interior and the U.S. Department of Justice. I was taught in my early career by some of the best lawyers I have ever met and I remain very proud of my years of government service. I continue to work with government lawyers with consummate skills. Nonetheless, not having paying clients and not being subject to the same type of malpractice exposure that exists in the private sector simply creates a different practice environment.

In my experience, government lawyers are exposed to a much broader range of issues and are thrust into "interesting" lawyering situations more often and at a much earlier stage in their careers than are their counterparts in the private sector. While this may have some significant drawback for the government "client," it provides an invaluable experience for the lawyer.

Additionally, for the lawyer who wishes to specialize in an area such as environmental law, there simply is no place where you can replicate the type of intense exposure to the nuances of this type of practice than through government service within an agency that focuses on these types of issues.

Federal Government Practice

As noted earlier, outside of the area of tort law (and, indeed, even with respect to much of that law), environmental law is predominantly statutory and regulatory in nature. For historic reasons, most of this statutory law began at the federal level. Initially, federal environmental law deferred to the states. The states, in turn, relied for the most part upon common law theories to deal with the remediation of identified concerns. In large part, this meant that private parties, through private civil litigation, attempted to abate nuisances or obtain damages for specified and individualized injury. The realization that significant environmental problems existed and needed to be dealt with through a broad-based approach did not take full flight until the late 1960s and early 1970s when environmental crises, from Love Canal to burning rivers and poison air, forced upon us a recognition that the existing "private" approach to environmental protection was not working. The consequence of this recognition was the development at the federal level of a broad-based statutory structure—starting with NEPA's directive to evaluate all major federal actions based upon their potential environmental impacts, to the more specific and focused directives contained within statutes such as the CWA, CAA, CERCLA, and RCRA, and their accompanying complex and technical regulations. These statutes not only contained civil sanctions for violations, but also included potential criminal penalties for knowing or grossly negligent violations of the statutory and regulatory mandates.

In this context, the EPA became the main focus of implementation and enforcement. However, because all federal agencies were the subject of these provisions, each agency of the federal government also needed to have in-house legal expertise to ensure compliance with these provisions. Notably, among these are the agencies within the Department of Defense and the Department of Energy, which have unique and complex environmental compliance problems. Additionally, the Department of Justice became involved with criminal enforcement actions. This includes the lawyers who work for the Department of Justice in Washington, D.C., as well as the various U.S. Attorneys' offices throughout the United States. The net result of this is that the federal government is fertile ground for someone who desires to enter the field of environmental law.

As a practical matter, you can divide the areas of environmental practice that can be engaged in at the federal governmental level into nine fairly distinct areas.

1. Governmental lawyers work as congressional staff assisting in the development of legislation. This work provides a mix of technical knowledge with a knowledge of applicable legal standards. The success of much environmental legislation is in its practical utility in the context of the legal system.

    There are really two different types of opportunities in this area. The first is the opportunity associated with working on the staff of an individual member of Congress. This type of work focuses on assisting with environmental issues associated with a member's committee assignments or with responding to individual constituent concerns.

    A second opportunity is presented as a committee staff member associated with a committee that has specific responsibilities with respect to environmental or related laws. This type of work requires, or in the course of the work itself develops, a degree of expertise that in some instances is quite unique. Understanding the ins and outs of environmental legislation and the process by which it is developed is often indispensable later in dealing with its implementation.

2. Government lawyers work within regulatory agencies assisting in all aspects of the development of needed rules and regulations. In addition to understanding the technical issues that underlie the regulatory structure, these lawyers must also ensure that applicable procedural requirements are adhered to. In addition, first-line challenges to environmental rules and regulations are often dealt with by these environmental lawyers. Government lawyers may also assist in the development of policies that as a practical matter become as important as statutory provisions or formal regulations.

3. Government lawyering, at the agency level, involves or includes assisting with what is needed to ensure compliance with environmental statutes and regulations. This might include assisting other agency personnel in the general permitting process, providing advice and assistance to agency staff on related legal issues, or meeting with individuals from the private sector and providing them with information on what they need to ensure compliance. Government lawyers at the agency level are also involved in the front line of environmental enforcement. Many environmental statutes have administrative sanctions that can be levied by the agency in the context of a quasi-judicial process.

4. Government lawyers at the agency level also provide support in civil and criminal litigation that may be initiated by the Department of Justice. These lawyers act as the liaison between the agency and the Department of Justice and in environmental cases often act "of counsel" to the Department of Justice, providing litigation support and assistance. This tends to round out the government's litigation team, with the agency lawyer providing substantive knowledge to the effort and ensuring that agency policy, with respect to the statutory or regulatory provision involved, is carried out.

5. Federal agencies are also subject to federal, state, and local environmental statutes and regulations. Lawyers representing government agencies, therefore, are involved in compliance and broader representational work similar to that which lawyers in the private sector face.

   Most typically, this type of agency work is outside the so-called regulatory agencies. The best example might be Department of Defense lawyers who must provide legal support for operations needed to maintain a given government installation. Those facilities need to proceed through the same kind of regulatory rigor as any private installation or facility (although a national defense exemption might apply in any given situation). This would include compliance with all of the various toxic and hazardous substance laws, compliance with the Clean Water Act and the Clean Air Act, the need to undertake NEPA review (including the drafting of environmental impact statements), and compliance with the provisions of the Endangered Species Act.

6. Lawyers within the Department of Defense and the Department of Energy, as noted earlier, must deal with unique problems associated with the cleanup of federal sites that have particularly pernicious toxics and hazardous substance problems. This work requires a specialized knowledge of the substance of the law. In addition, it requires a type of real-world application of the statutory and regulatory provisions of the law as intense as you are likely to see anywhere.

7. Lawyers within the Department of the Interior, the Department of Agriculture, and the National Marine Fisheries Service deal on a routine basis with the general type of matters that are dealt with by lawyers representing any regulatory agency. In administering statutes like the Endangered Species Act, Marine Mammal Protection Act, the various wilderness and roadless statutes, Wild and Scenic Rivers Act provisions, as well as statutes associated with the general administration of the public lands, including national parks, national forests, timber statutes, grazing statutes, federal water-related statues, the mineral laws (including the Hard Rock Mining Law of 1872), the various mineral leasing acts, and the Surface Mining Control and Reclamation Act, these lawyers are called upon to undertake all of the roles of a regulatory lawyer. This includes the drafting of legislation and proposed regulations, ensuring that the regulatory process is adhered to both in actual rulemaking and thereafter. This work, of course, also involves general compliance and permitting issues and, where necessary, enforcement. Enforcement may include involvement in administrative penalty phases and administrative hearings, as well as providing assistance to the Department of Justice in the case of civil or criminal enforcement actions.

These agencies also have extensive internal appeal processes that must be followed in order to exhaust administrative remedies in any challenge to agency decision making. Agency lawyers are utilized to defend the government's position and are also utilized as hearing officers, on appeal. In most of these administrative agencies there has been generated a large body of internal decisions, on administrative appeal, with which you must become familiar.

In addition to the administration of the agency's own statutory and regulatory provisions, these agencies, similar to the Department of Defense, operate facilities and implement programs throughout the United States. These facilities and programs are all subject to the same environmental statutory and regulatory limits that constrain private activities. This means that the agency lawyer must assist the agency in compliance with environmental laws, including the various permitting requirements that may be implicated in any given situation. Interestingly enough, among the environmental statutory and regulatory schemes that need to be adhered to are statutes, such as the Endangered Species Act, that other lawyers within the same agency are charged with implementing. Thus, lawyers from the same agency may sit on opposite sides of the table, both representing the same client but wearing the different hats of the agency. This type of experience is obviously unique and also provides a type of experience that does not (cannot) exist elsewhere.

8. As noted above, agency lawyers are also involved in the administrative hearing process involved in the implementation of most, if not all, of the statutory and regulatory provisions that may be implicated in this area of the law. This is not a minor area. Also, as noted above, most of the agencies that are even remotely implicated in this area of the law have extensive internal administrative review processes. Usually the process begins with the decision of the agency head or delegated personnel. This decision, once made, may be the subject of several levels of appeal, each of which requires or involves some level of legal brief-

ing and advocacy. In some instances the review process can be very formal, including the involvement of an administrative law judge as, for example, are land-related decisions within the Department of the Interior where appeals are heard by the Interior Board of Land Appeals. In each of these situations agency lawyers are called upon to defend the agency position. This requires (or develops) a fairly strong foundation not only in the substance of the law that is involved, but also with administrative process and procedures. Since the appeal is required in order to exhaust all administrative remedies, it is a mandatory stop on the way to dealing with any challenged agency action. Intimate knowledge of this type of situation is invaluable in a successful practice.

In addition to this type of work, the various environmental statutes have provisions for the imposition of administrative penalties. These provisions were intended to provide enforcement flexibility to agencies that would avoid the need for obtaining judicial resolution and Department of Justice assistance in every environmental enforcement situation. This type of process, of course, has also required the development of additional skills and knowledge on the part of agency lawyers who must negotiate with individuals and entities who are subject to administrative enforcement actions and, if unsuccessful in negotiation, proceed through the "prosecution" side of the administrative action.

9. In addition to the general agency work identified above, lawyers within the U.S. Department of Justice and in the various U.S. Attorneys' offices have the primary responsibility to represent the United States in civil and criminal judicial proceedings associated with the enforcement and, in some cases as—for example, with respect to citizen suits—defense of the United States in environmental litigation. This type of work requires that government lawyers become familiar with all aspects of the laws that they will need to litigate. This, of course, includes a thorough knowledge of the statutory and regulatory provisions that are

implicated. It also involves an understanding of the technical issues that are involved in or underlying the law itself. In addition, depending on the nature of the litigation involved, other specialized knowledge needs to be developed.

For example, in the situation where an agency action (or inaction) is at issue, the litigating lawyer must also have a working knowledge of the administrative process that led to the decision that is at issue. Procedural issues, such as the appropriate standard or scope of review, may be as important or more important than the substance of the dispute.

In enforcement actions, understanding agency policy and past actions may be of crucial importance in determining how to proceed. Working closely with the agency and its lawyers is essential in this regard. Also because criminal enforcement is, in fact, criminal law, understanding how to proceed in that regard is essential.

The bottom line here is that in addition to having the substantive and procedural knowledge associated with the underlying environmental laws that are at issue, Department of Justice lawyers and lawyers with the United States Attorneys' office must also have the underlying procedural and substantive knowledge needed to litigate. The benefit of working for the government in this area is that there are few, if any, situations within the private sector where you are exposed to as much focused environmental litigation as is available in government service.

State Government Practice

An important aspect of the overarching federal statutory and regulatory presence in this area of the law is a delegation to the states of environmental regulation. The federal law allows state implementation of many of these statutes so long as the states have adopted a statutory structure that is at least as stringent as that provided by federal law. Not wanting the federal government to control how individuals and entities operate within it, states have been zealous in enacting statutory and regulatory programs that meet the federal stringency requirements. In general, the EPA has been given the role of reviewing and certifying these state programs as meeting the requirements of the federal law and, where appropriate, delegating implementation and enforcement authority to the states. Thus, state government provides another area for employment, both in enforcement, through state agencies delegated the responsibility under state implementation statutes to implement these environmental programs, as well as the states attorneys general offices that are responsible for enforcement. Moreover, as is the case with respect to federal agencies, the state and its instrumentalities are subject to these environmental laws and, as a consequence, environmental compliance expertise is needed throughout state government. For the most part, the federal agencies noted earlier each have their state counterpart.

Examples of state counterparts of the federal agency involvement include the following:

1. Departments of ecology or environmental protection exist on the state level. These agencies, more or less, mirror the responsibility of the EPA. At the state level, however, many of the EPA functions are sub-delegated to specific agencies within these departments or, in some cases, to separate agencies or departments. Nonetheless, you should be able to find state agencies with parallel responsibilities in specific resource or statutory areas. Work in these agencies includes assistance in the drafting and updating of legislative and regulatory provisions at issue, as well as guiding the agency in keeping abreast of the changes in congressional and EPA policy and direction. Agency lawyers in this regard must not only focus on their own actions and the actions of the State Legislature, but be concerned with ensuring that state law and the agency's programs remain in compliance with federal law. State agency lawyers may need to also become involved, on behalf of the state, in the parallel federal process in order to ensure that the state's position and programs are known and protected.

   State agency lawyers must also be familiar with state procedural requirements and be able to guide the agency in its rulemaking through these processes. Once in place, lawyers must assist with permitting and other compliance-related work. This work also must be undertaken with at least one eye toward the federal programs and processes that parallel the state's.

Challenges to agency decision making and enforcement actions will involve the state agency lawyers in administrative appeals similar to what exists on the federal level. How a state deals with these challenges and enforcement also may have ramifications with respect to parallel federal programs. As a consequence, state agency lawyers may need to coordinate with their federal counterparts.

2. Additionally, there are state agencies responsible for the natural resources and other environmental areas discussed earlier. For example, there are state departments of forestry, state departments of game and fish, and state park departments. Lawyers within these departments assist in the administration of state programs in these areas in a manner similar to what is done on the federal level. These lawyers must be able to administer the statutory and regulatory provisions associated with their departments, assist in administering department programs, and also ensure that those provisions of state law comply with environmental contracts and requirements of federal law. Again, the state lawyer has a coordination role that does not necessarily exist on the federal level.

3. State agencies, just like federal agencies, are responsible for insuring that their department's activities and actions comply with applicable statutory and regulatory provisions. In the case of state departments, this includes compliance with all applicable federal laws and all applicable state laws. This may, in any given situation, be a much broader requirement than what federal lawyers need to deal with.

4. The state attorneys general offices serve a similar role to that of the Department of Justice and the U.S. Attorneys' office, although in some states exclusive representation in litigation is not reserved to the attorneys general and, as a

consequence, some agency lawyers may have a litigation function. Again, the state attorneys involved will often need to coordinate with their federal counterparts.

Local Government Practice

As was the case with respect to federal delegation to the states, enforcement and compliance work also trickles down to local government. In many situations enforcement and first-tier regulation associated with environmental statutes vests in city or county health departments and with local district attorneys charged with criminal enforcement.

Work in this area will also include dealing with local land-use decision making. This involves dealing not only with the whole host of issues noted above, but also with zoning and other related regulations of a purely local nature.

Also, as was the case with respect to federal and state compliance, local agencies of the state must themselves comply with state and federal environmental statutory and regulatory provisions. As a consequence, local government provides a fertile field for the development of the lawyering skills needed to pursue more focused environmental law employment.

Examples of local counterparts to the federal and state representational areas noted above include the following:

1. At the city and county level, offices of the city attorney or county counsel handle much of the legal work within all of the various city or county departments. This would include legal work related to local land-use planning, which by nature includes a great deal of environmental-related review, including review of zoning-related issues, and ensuring that the city or county approvals themselves comply with state and federal environmental law. General plan adoption and approvals, for example, require a broad array of environmental considerations, not the least of which includes considerations associated with open space, Endangered Species Act compliance, Clean Water Act approvals, and Clean Air Act approvals.

In addition to developing necessary ordinances and regulations to implement city or county policy direction in these areas, city attorney and county counsel offices need to ensure that the various related approvals and permitting are conducted in an appropriate fashion and, where necessary, that routine enforcement occurs. Lawyerys within these offices also have obligations and responsibilities to defend these entities from challenges to city or county decision making.

2. Departments of public health need lawyer assistance and involvement in compliance and enforcement work. This type of work is similar to that which is undertaken by EPA lawyers at the state and federal levels. This type of work is primarily in the context of first promulgating and then implementing and enforcing regulations.

3. Also, at this level of government, many departments are routinely involved in environmental issues. These departments include utility departments that operate solid-waste disposal facilities, water-treatment facilities, and waste-water-treatment facilities. Work in these local departments will include the drafting of rules and regulations associated with the utilization of these systems and facilities, and ensuring that customers remain in compliance.

    In addition, the activities engaged in by these departments are heavily regulated themselves. Clean Water Act and Safe Drinking Water Act permitting and compliance is fairly significant work that must be undertaken by lawyers representing these entities. This involves issues from routine compliance and the permitting of these facilities to representation of departments in administrative and judicial forums. Facilities operated by these departments are also a prime target of citizen suits that require lawyers to represent these agencies in these types of actions.

4. Most of the city and county ordinances and regulatory provisions include some type of sanctioning provision that is triggered if the ordinances or regulations are violated. Some of these sanctions are fairly modest and are imposed administratively; some, however, are more onerous and

include some kind of judicial involvement. In these types of situations the local district attorneys offices are most often involved in the initiation and the prosecution of environmental crimes.

Additionally, while the state attorneys general often prosecute environmental crimes, the bulk of these prosecutions at the criminal level are undertaken at the local level through work undertaken by local district attorneys.

5. In addition to city and county opportunities, there are numerous other local governmental agencies that require routine environmental legal services. These entities range from mosquito abatement districts to water districts or special districts that might, for example, undertake local utility services. Indeed, in some situations, because of the focused nature of the work involved, the amount of involvement in environmental issues far exceeds that which might exist at the city or county level. The work that is involved here may include the entire range of issues that would otherwise be faced by the city or county government lawyers representing individual utility departments. While many of these entities retain private legal counsel, many are large enough to retain in-house legal counsel.

Public Advocacy Legal Work

As noted above, environmental law has different connotations depending upon whom you are dealing with. The environmental advocate may have a very different perspective on the enactment and implementation of environmental laws and regulations than one within the regulated community. Moreover, views on the ends of this continuum are fairly strong. As a consequence, there is an extensive array of paid professionals and volunteers working as advocates of a diverse range of environmental positions. These may include groups like the Natural Resources Defense Council (NRDC) and Environmental Defense Fund (EDF) on one hand, and the Pacific Legal Foundation (PLF) and Mountain States Legal Foundation (MSLF) on the other. They may also include any number of more focused groups concerned with some particular environmental interests or even associations that follow the environmental regulations associated with a particular industry.

This work involves legislative advocacy, research, and writing within the area of environmental law, commenting on the development of regulations, and perhaps the challenge of those regulations. Indeed, much of the early development and amplification in the area of environmental law was facilitated by the environmental, legislative advocacy of these groups and in the litigation these entities initiated to ensure the proper implementation and then enforcement of the law. Even today this type of litigation is still pursued with lawsuits, particularly involving policy and related issues associated with the administration of the public lands and decisions associated with listing under and administration of the ESA the most prominent.

For the most part, however, a great deal of this type of work has shifted toward the area of general policy making with a great deal of time and effort being spent in the pursuit of legal mechanisms that will better effectuate desired ends and in the participation, as stakeholders, in consensus-building efforts. Indeed, environmental law has developed a whole new array of options associated with implementation and enforcement that revolves around the development of consensus among all interested parties. Whether this is a good or bad development in the law is yet to be seen. Nonetheless, consensus building is time intensive and provides a very large and potentially effective role for the public advocacy lawyer.

In addition, most of the environmental statutes contain within them a citizen-suit provision allowing any person the right to sue in order to force compliance. These private attorney-general actions have given birth to an entire specialized area of litigation that, in addition to having the potential of forcing compliance, also contain the prospect of civil penalties being assessed against the defendant(s) and an attorneys' fee awarded to the environmental plaintiff. Over the years this type of litigation has served various purposes, some useful, some not. Regardless of your view on this issue, there is no question that these provisions have spawned a whole new opportunity for lawyers to both support themselves as well as organizations with whom they are affiliated.

Corporate Environmental Law

Large corporations also need and have developed extensive in-house expertise in the area of environmental law. This expertise is needed to follow potential legislation that might affect the business interests of the corporation and to participate in rulemaking, which will to a very large degree control how business can and will be undertaken.

Small businesses, of course, also need to be concerned about and involved in this legislative and regulatory process. As a consequence, most industries have formed associations that, through the pooling of resources, can represent the interests of an entire industry, including the interests of smaller businesses. These associations also have the ability to seek out and coordinate their activities with other associations representing different industries that may, nonetheless, have similar concerns about proposed or actual statutory or regulatory provisions. Association representation provides various opportunities for lawyers seeking experience in environmental law.

In addition to this type of general advocacy, lawyers within corporations or associations need to be able to assist their clients in all of the various compliance work that exists. This work may run the entire length of environmental law and include local permitting and zoning issues, as well as proceeding through the state and federal statutory and regulatory maze. Once up and running, representation will include ensuring that all of the corporation's operations remain in compliance with applicable local, state. and federal environmental mandates.

Finally, in-house counsel must and often do either directly represent their clients in litigation or act as liaison between the client and outside legal counsel. This representation will include not only understanding the basic legal concepts that may be involved, but also understanding the nuances of corporate obligations and responsibility for environmental compliance and the potential exposure of directors, officers, and employees of the corporation. These types of issues and their interrelationship have an amazing impact on how businesses and individuals within businesses may make crucial decisions.

Again, these areas offer another avenue of employment for the environmental lawyer and, similar to the other areas outside of the private practice sector noted above, may provide the environmental level lawyer with even more fertile ground in which to grow.

Developing a Private Environmental Law Practice

4

IT IS VERY DIFFICULT TO BUILD an environmental law practice from scratch, and only marginally easier to shift an existing, more general practice into one that specializes in environmental law. At the heart of this point is that in order to have a successful environmental law practice, you need to have an environmental lawyer. To be an environmental lawyer requires a great deal more than the taking of environmental classes in law school. It requires, in addition to the academic knowledge of the substantive area of practice, gaining practical experience. There are any number of avenues for gaining this experience. In my view and from my experience, the best way and perhaps the easiest is to work for one or more of the various administrative agencies that are charged with administering the law. In this regard, and as noted earlier, the EPA, Department of the Interior, Department of the Army, Department of Energy, and Department of Justice, to name only a few, and their state and local counterparts have been the training ground for countless successful environmental lawyers. There are few people who know the ins and outs of their respective

45

areas of practice better than lawyers who were once charged with the responsibility of administering the statutes and regulations at issue. Not only do they know the law, but they know the procedures and the people who administer the law. In this regard, people with this type of experience begin their private practice with a head start that is often difficult to overcome.

Other significant considerations underscoring the difficulty in starting an environmental law practice are the more technical aspects of this area of practice and its interface with the nonlegal professionals who are also involved in environmental issues. In order to gain entry into this world, you almost need to have a guide through the complex statutory and regulatory structure, as well as to become familiar with the various administrative agency procedures and agency personalities. Indeed, as will be discussed later, it is even helpful to have a guide shepherd you through all of the conferencing that is endemic in this area of practice, since attendance and participation at these gatherings is essential to success.

There are, of course, other avenues available to gain experience. For lawyers who want to strike out on their own at some point in time, working for firms with existing environmental law practices or within corporations with environmental sections are also means to gain the requisite level of experience. Another means to obtain experience is through working for environmental advocacy groups.

For existing firms that wish to expand their practice into the area of environmental law, two possible avenues exist. The first is to hire laterally a lawyer with the requisite level of experience and around whom the environmental part of the practice can be built. This is the most certain and quickest way to the development of a successful practice. A second, less certain means is to attempt to enter the area more slowly, allowing a lawyer on staff the time—a great deal of time—to learn the ropes through trial and error. At one time, when the field of practice was first evolving, this was perhaps the more usual means through which a practice could be developed. At that time, however, everyone was learning and learning together, and as a consequence, it was not possible to find the experienced practitioner. That situation, of course, has changed and proceeding in this manner may put your firm at a competitive disadvantage that it may not be able to overcome.

Proceeding in either way, or at all, has its own considerations. Some of these are client related and some are purely economic. At one time the supply of environmental lawyers was so limited and the demand so great that there was hardly any risk in embarking on an environmental law practice or expanding into these areas. There is a general perception that this is still the case; however, it is not. Today things are quite different from the way they once were, and competition is intense.

This, of course, does not mean that a successful practice cannot be initiated. It just means that you need to proceed from a proper perspective and evaluate how to proceed based upon a real-world understanding of what may be faced.

In this context, client expectations need also to be considered. At one time clients expected to pay a great deal for the expertise of the limited number of lawyers that practiced environmental law. In some situations this is still true, but for the most part, this is no longer the case. Most major sources of clients, where the bulk of the work resides, include individuals or entities who have factored environmental compliance into their business planning and who now want what they perceive to be routine matters dealt with at a routine price. This means that they are willing to shop around for lawyers who will undertake the work involved for a lower price. In any given situation this may be acceptable, particularly since the tradeoff is a higher volume of work than otherwise would be available.

I once represented a very large multinational client in matters associated with petroleum-related contamination. While these matters can be fairly routine, the specific assignments I was provided all had unique elements associated with them. I did a great job, resolving in litigation, through settlement, multiple issues that under the same situation would have taken years and involved dozens of lawyers. Nonetheless, when the client reorganized, it wanted me to adjust my higher rate downward toward the rate it paid lawyers who dealt with the routine matters. The client, as an incentive, offered to also provide me with more of this type of routine work with which I could train new associates. I refused. What was being offered just was not the type of practice that I wanted. The client, as a consequence, went elsewhere where it obtained the rate that it wanted.

You must ask whether what is offered is the type of practice you want to have. If the rate, for example, is not what you want, then you need to seek out the more specialized areas of environmental law where higher fees may be commanded. These types of matters, of course, may also have their own pitfalls. You need to consider the risks associated with representing the client that does not view environmental compliance as routine. You must question why this is the case and whether there are more significant problems yet to be uncovered than the ones that are known.

Reasonable expectations on both the part of the client and the lawyer are essential. A lawyer needs to ensure that he or she is not confronted with having to surprise a client with the message about the nature of the problem involved, as well as the potential costs—including attorneys' fees—that may need to be addressed in order to cure the problem. While this type of work may be potentially lucrative, in the end the client may not be able to withstand the risk and expense of what is necessary for compliance. While the potential for economic reward in these types of cases is great, the risk that your client may not be able to pay is an equal possibility. In this regard, you will want to ask if this is the type of practice that you want to have.

Between these two extremes, of course, is a range of possible situations. You need to consider carefully exactly what you are looking for and what is realistically available in order to make intelligent decisions on how to proceed.

In any event, the point is that you need to understand your motivation for entering this area of the law. Do you wish to enter to serve an existing client need, or because you wish to attempt to expand your area of practice into what appears to be a potentially lucrative field? Once these questions are answered, questions of an economic nature should be addressed. What costs are associated with a lateral hire versus the in-house development of the requisite expertise? These cost considerations should not only include consideration of salaries and overhead, but also should consider the time that you anticipate will be needed in order to develop business. The following are some of the more specific questions that should be addressed.

Qustions to Ask About Establishing an Environmental Law Practice

1. What, if any, practical background in environmental law or any of the associated technical fields do you have or exists within the pool of lawyers that wish to begin the practice? To the extent this background exists, what environmental focus will the practice take on?

2. What means do you intend to employ to obtain the requisite expertise or skill needed to, as a practical matter, practice in this area? Do you intend to learn by doing? Do you intend to learn through association with other lawyers who practice in this area?

3. As part of your business plan, how much time have you planned for in the development of your client base? While practical skills can, of course, be learned by doing, proceeding in this manner will almost by necessity limit the number of clients that you can represent. Do you have the economic resources to proceed in this manner?

4. Are there other firms with an existing environmental practice with which you an associate? Can they provide you with clients and assist in educating you with respect to practical skills?

5. Are there other areas of practice that you can undertake as your environmental practice is developing? In other words, are you willing to begin the practice of environmental law in phases, rather than all at once?

6. Can you identify technical experts whom you can rely upon to assist you in understanding pitfalls and the broader ramifications of the practice? Can you take the time to attend and afford the expense of practice-based conferences focused on environmental law?

Questions to Ask About Lateral Hiring

1. What focus do you intend to place on the environmental practice? Will this focus serve the needs of existing clients

and if so, how? Can and how will the environmental practice integrate with the existing practice?

2. What salary is intended for the lateral hire?

3. How many additional lawyers are available or is the firm willing to hire in order to support work generated by the lateral hire? Over what period of time will this occur?

4. What general overhead is to be allocated to this lawyer or lawyers and how long do you expect it to take before this lawyer will be able to cover this overhead? What is the anticipated time needed to build the practice to a level in which the lawyers involved will be able to bill a substantial amount of time to the environmental practice? In the interim, will those lawyers be able to work on other legal work within the firm?

5. What costs are there associated with conferences and related technical meetings?

6. What costs are there associated with the extra marketing involved in the shift to or addition of an environmental law practice?

7. What costs are there associated with the acquisition of resource materials such as treatises and informative newsletters?

8. What "spin-off" work is expected from the core environmental practice? Can the firm undertake this work or will it refer this work to others?

9. What, if any, conflicts or other ethical issues are likely to arise in the context of a shift to or the addition of an environmental law practice?

Questions to Ask About Using Lawyers Currently On Staff

1. What focus do you intend to place on the environmental practice? Will this focus serve the needs of existing clients and if so, how? Can and how will the environmental practice integrate with the existing practice?

2. What salary is intended or exists for the lawyer or lawyers who are to be involved in the environmental law practice?

3. What general firm overhead is allocated to this lawyer or lawyers? How long do you anticipate before the environmental practice will need to cover this overhead?

4. What amount of current billable time will be needed to be redirected toward environmental law practice development? How much time will be needed to be devoted to an existing nonenvironmental law practice?

5. How many additional lawyers are available or is the firm willing to hire in order to support work generated by this new practice emphasis? Over what period of time will this occur?

6. What is the anticipated time needed to build the practice to a level in which the lawyer or lawyers involved will be able to bill a substantial amount of time to the environmental practice?

7. What costs are there associated with conferences and related technical meetings?

8. What costs are there associated with the extra marketing involved in the shift to or addition of an environmental law practice?

9. What costs are there associated with the acquisition of resource materials such as treatises and informational newsletters?

10. What "spin-off" work is expected from the core environmental practice? Can the firm undertake this work or will it refer this work to others?

11. What, if any, conflicts or other ethical issues are likely to arise in the context of a shift to or the addition of an environmental law practice?

Managing Your Private Practice 5

ASSUMING YOU HAVE TACKLED the fundamental and central task of developing and accounting for basic environmental lawyer expertise and skills—in other words, you are competent to practice in the area of environmental law—the next question to deal with is the nature of the practice that you wish to have. Most of these issues are similar, if not the same, to those presented when you start any law firm. The establishment of an environmental law practice, however, may present twists to these basic issues of concern that are more or less unique. In starting an environmental law practice, the general rules apply, with perhaps the following concerns deserving some additional consideration: what your environmental law firm should look like; the retention agreement; alternative forms of agreement; types of billing; space considerations; your law library; technology issues; support staff; continuing legal education; and the business aspects of the environmental law practice. This chapter discusses each of these topics in turn.

What Should Your Environmental Law Firm Look Like?

How many lawyers do you want to have?

There are successful solo environmental practices and there are successful small, mid-sized, and large environmental law practices. There is no reason to believe that one form of practice is inherently better than another. However, while the question of the size of a practice may ultimately be answered based upon personal preferences, there are issues specific to the environmental law practice that should be considered in the beginning.

Solo Practice?

Any one environmental law case or client can be very time consuming. Indeed, it is possible that over a long period of time a lawyer would need to focus only on the needs of one client. In this context, the economics of the practice need to be considered. A linear practice, involving only one lawyer, in which you can focus on one client's work until completion and then move to another may be desirable, but not realistic. A solo practitioner focusing on only one client's work has any number of downsides. For one thing, focusing all of your energy on one case runs the risk of finding no work ready for you when you have completed your current case. No matter how good you are, if you are not available, clients and their business will go elsewhere. Additionally, you need to remember that not all clients pay for services timely, or at all. A focus on undertaking poor-paying clients' work can be disastrous to a solo practice that focuses on one or a limited number of clients at a time.

In reality, a solo practice simply cannot focus exclusively on one client unless some consideration of these underlying concerns is factored into firm economics and income expectations. Alternatively, the nature of the practice will need to be limited to those types of "bite-sized" issues that do not take an extensive commitment of time.

If a solo practice does not work, how large a practice is needed to be able to effectively practice environmental law?

I have practiced in a firm with in excess of one-hundred lawyers and a start-up firm of about six lawyers that has, to date, grown to a firm of about fifteen lawyers who all specialize in some area of environmental law. I have enjoyed the actual practice of law in all of these settings. My preference with respect to size has, in fact, more to do with the type of life I wish to lead than the nature of the practice itself. However, the need to be able to meet the needs of my clients, while at the same time maintaining firm economics that allow for economic viability, mandates a certain realistic approach to the question of minimum size. It is in this context that it appears to me that the more efficient and effective environmental law practice begins with more than one lawyer and builds from that point based upon a whole host of considerations, most of which are rooted in personal preferences.

Scope of Substantive and Other Coverage and Its Relationship to Firm Growth

How large a firm is allowed to grow involves any number of variables, including, of course, preference. A successful firm's size, however, may, in fact, be difficult to control. In this regard, I do not here want to focus on the question of lifestyle and personal preferences, which are dealt with in more general treatments of this topic, but rather to focus on a related question that may bear on the ultimate question of size and that does that in the context of an environmental law practice. In order to grapple with this issue, various questions should be addressed:

1. What kind of coverage do you intend for your practice?
2. Do you intend to focus on one or more specific areas of environmental law?
3. Do you intend to focus on a broad base of services within the environmental specialty, including, for example, regulatory work, compliance, and transactional work? Do you intend to litigate? If so, will you focus on litigation at the

administrative level? Will you include judicial litigation as part of your practice?

4. In the alternative, will you sub-specialize in your environmental practice focusing on either limited substantive areas or limited practice areas within either a limited or broad-based environmental practice?

5. Do you intend to provide legal services outside of the field of environmental law? If so, will this offering complement the environmental law practice? Will it be integrated with the environmental law practice? Will it be independent of the environmental law practice?

As noted earlier, the practice of environmental law means a lot of things to a lot of people. Perhaps the best way to grapple with the question of size is to first answer some of these questions about the scope of your intended environmental practice.

Focus on a More Finite Aspect of Environmental Law

One option that clearly presents itself is to focus on some finite aspect of environmental law. This way of proceeding itself presents a number of options. You could focus on a very narrow aspect of environmental law. For example, you might decide to only undertake legislative advocacy and to further focus by limiting your advocacy to only one or two specific areas, such as clean water or clean air.

Another example might include a focus on a litigation practice and, to be even more focused, on a litigation practice that brings only citizen suits, with compensation based upon awards of lawyers' fees. Indeed, the focus can be even greater to a litigation practice that only undertakes citizen suits on the CWA or the ESA or other specific statutes.

The ability to focus, in this regard, really embraces two options: the ability to focus on a specific statute; or, in the alternative, the ability to focus on one aspect of the general statutory or regulatory structure that might be common to many different statutes. Thus, for example, you might be able to focus on regulatory programs or the drafting of certain types of transactional documents, ensuring that certain types of compliance work are undertaken.

Another option with respect to focus might be to become expert with respect to all aspects of a specific statute or resource area. For example, you could decide to focus on "water" as a practice area and offer representation in all matters associated with water regardless of how it presented itself. As a consequence, you would undertake representation of matters associated with the resource itself (particularly in the Western water-rights context) or, with respect to pollution-driven questions such as those that might be presented under the CWA or the SDWA. You might also provide representation in the area of wetland regulation, ESA issues, and the whole array of other "environmental" issues associated with the ecology of water. This type of focus would afford you the ability to specialize, while still enjoying the ability to utilize a broad array of skills.

Viewed in this way, the various environmental-law-practice options that you may have are almost unlimited, but because ultimately there is a narrow focus, you will be able to better control the size of your practice. These types of more focused options may best fit the needs of a solo firm or small practice. This type of focus allows a limited number of lawyers to undertake an extensive amount of work. Moreover, there is a real market for this type of specialized practice. The hard part is clearly defining the scope of the practice so that the focus can serve as a marketing tool.

Remember, the skills needed to practice environmental law are almost as diverse as the law itself. Addressing the question of whether you are to be a transactional law firm, a litigation law firm, or attempt to do both, and every other aspect of your decision with respect to specialization will also have broad ramifications with respect to the size of your firm. The less focused you want to be, the more you should be concerned about how you intend to meet the diverse needs of more than one client over time.

The Broad-Based Environmental Practice

Focusing on the scope of your practice is the most effective way to control size. Alternative models that allow for larger growth also include the ability to provide a more diverse mix of environmental practice areas to prospective clients. This can be accomplished in various ways, but two more fundamental models may be helpful for the purpose of this discussion.

The first is one in which the firm is divided into practice areas. In this type of model, certain lawyers focus on legislation, with others dealing with regulatory and compliance matters, and others with litigation. Within this model certain lawyers may be more substantively knowledgeable with respect to certain specific statutory or regulatory areas (such as clean air or clean water), but for the most part the firm's work is divided by practice areas, with the litigation involved in the litigation of clean-air-related matters on one day and RCRA matters on another. Since this type of firm is not limited in the number of clients to which it can provide legal services, limitation in growth, if any, is caused by the exercise of preferences and other practical limitations, including the success and economics of the practice.

The second model is one in which the firm is divided along resource or statutory lines, with certain lawyers dealing with all matters that might come into the firm associated with clean air and others dealing with clean-water issues. There may also be within the firm litigation experts or experts in various transactional matters, but the primary division of work is divided along statutory or resource lines. Again, since this type of firm is not limited in the number of clients to which it can provide legal services, limitation in growth, if any, is caused by the exercise of preferences and other practical limitations, including the success and economics of the practice.

In either of these two models, or in any other firm that specializes exclusively in environmental law, some consideration should be given to how to handle the spin-off, nonenvironmental, legal work that will invariably come your way. Two obvious options exist. First, you can arrange to and associate with either specialized firms that can undertake the nonenvironmental work that needs to be undertaken; or you can decide to accommodate these clients within the firm. Proceeding in the former way requires some consideration of the arrangement you desire with the other firm, if any. These considerations include whether you want, if permissible, a fee-sharing arrangement or other economic credit for the work to be undertaken; or whether you want the other firm to bill through you in the nature of a cost that will be passed on to the client. Proceeding in this way implicates certain ethical and insurance issues that are not involved in a simple referral.

Proceeding in the latter manner and accommodating the work yourself requires you to consider the ramifications of this decision. At the forefront of this is the question of how many areas outside of environmental law will you be able or willing to expand into? Will you need to add corporate, tax, or real estate lawyers to the firm? If so, what consequences will this have to the nature of the practice? Will it transform the practice from its specialty area because of the need to continually find clients and work to keep these nonenvironmental lawyers busy; or will they also become environmental lawyers? What consequence will all of this have to the size of the firm and an ability to control growth?

These are not easy questions and how they are answered means a lot with respect to the type of law practice that you ultimately have. You should grapple with these questions early and make decisions up-front on your intentions. Not doing so will result in unplanned and unintended limitations or expansion in firm growth, as well as changes in the nature of your practice that may affect the quality of practice or life that you otherwise had in mind.

The Broad-Based Practice That Includes Representation in the Area of Environmental Law

The last option that should be discussed is the environmental practice that is a part of a larger, more general law practice. This type of practice can be constituted based upon any of the models noted above. The firm could decide to limit its environmental practice in a focused manner with a few lawyers specializing in one of the ways discussed earlier. Moreover, this type of practice could be autonomous in nature, not relying upon other lawyers within the firm. The sole benefit that this type of limited environmental practice would have to the large firm would be in spin-off work in nonenvironmental legal fields.

A more typical way of proceeding, however, is one in which there is some integration with the rest of the firm. This can be an integration in which the environmental law specialty constitutes one department where they "borrow" lawyers with practice skills as they need them. Thus, at any given time the environmental lawyer may involve a tax specialist, a real estate specialist, and/or a litigation specialist on behalf of a single client with an environmental matter at issue. The environmental lawyer in this type of situation may manage the other lawyers and guide their work in order to ensure that all of the unique facets of environmental law are considered. In the alternative, it may be the tax lawyer, real estate lawyer, or litigator that involves the environmental lawyer as part of a team of lawyers who are working on a problem that has environmental issues involved.

Another variation on how a general practice firm could integrate its environmental practice is to have an environmental specialist within each of its practice areas. As a consequence, this type of firm might have real estate lawyers expert in various aspects of environmental law or environmental litigation within the litigation department.

Which of these models you adopt has a lot to do with how the general practice is otherwise organized. The goal, however, is to both integrate the environmental practice with the broader practice to ensure that all lawyers' time and skills are expended and utilized to the maximum degree and, at the same time, that the quality of client services is as high as possible; and to also be able to spread the benefits of spin-off work throughout the firm.

The Retention Agreement

I am always up-front with clients about the fees and costs that will be associated with the services that I provide. In this regard, I am candid about the fact that representing clients in environmental matters is expensive. I also indicate that while I can predict with accuracy some aspects of the fees and costs equation, I cannot predict them all. I note that this, in part, is due to the nature of environmental law and the fact that any number of factors outside of my control will dictate ultimate fees and costs. These outside considerations include: the physical facts that might present themselves in any given situation; the nature of third-party involvement; the involvement of regulatory agencies; and the potential for litigation. This candid approach serves to ensure to that there is no misunderstanding between lawyer and client about what is expected.

This initial discussion, of course, also encompasses a number of other matters of crucial concern. These matters, in addition to being part of client intake, should ultimately constitute the substance of crucial portions of the attorney–client retention agreement. This document, which may be required in some states, also serves to articulate the exact expectations that the lawyer should have of the client, and the client of the lawyer. While these arrangements are not unique to the environmental practice, there are perhaps some unique areas that should be covered. (See Appendix C for an example.)

The Business Deal

There must be an understanding and the fee agreements must articulate all aspects of the business part of the transaction. In other words, the agreement must contain specific terms dealing with billing rates, expected payment periods, costs, both extraordinary and routine, interest on overdue bills, and means of securing payment in the case of default. I discuss these and related issues later as part of a general discussion with respect to billing.

The Attorney–Client Relationship

The fee agreement should articulate simply the basic concept that the lawyer and client need to communicate with one another and that they need to be truthful with one another. It should also articulate the fact that in many situations the client will need to actively assist the lawyer in ensuring the best representation.

Scope of Work—Estimate of Time and Costs

I like to include within the agreement, or as an attachment to it, a fairly detailed description of the scope of work for which I have been retained. In many cases, the client presents a lot of information that together constitutes the "problem" that he or she wishes you to deal with. The client, however, has no idea exactly what needs to be done or the relative seriousness of what is presented. In other situations the client will drop on your desk a load of documents or other materials that was received from a regulatory agency and needs you to determine and then explain what it all means. In still other situations, the client will describe a course of business or other conduct that he or she wishes to engage in and requests that you provide advice on how best to proceed.

In all of these situations it is up to the lawyer to determine what needs to be done and then to clearly communicate these conclusions to the client. I use a detailed scope of work to do this. I first assess what I learned during my initial session with the client and my review of materials provided to me, and then attempt to articulate what needs to be done and the result that should be obtained if I am successful. I attempt to make this as detailed a description as is warranted in the given situation.

As part of the scope of work, I also like to describe how I will handle the matter, including a discussion of how much of my time will be involved in the representation and in what specific tasks and also who else will work on the matter and what they will do. In making these decisions I attempt to achieve the most efficient and cost-effective means of representation. Proceeding in this manner ought to allow you to assess time commitments that are being made, both in terms of the production of an ultimate product (if that is what is called for) or in terms of how much you will personally be involved in a matter. The idea is to provide realistic time projections and not to overcommit your own involvement. Adhering to these projections and using them as a means to avoid overcommitment of time is one of the most difficult and least successful things that I do. Nonetheless, the tool is there, and it should be used in order to avoid substantial problems as representation proceeds.

I also like to include overall timelines or estimates of the total time that will be needed. While this is not possible in all situations, where it is, it provides the client with a time context in order to understand the nature of what is being done. Also, if possible, I provide specific points within the timeline for consultation with the client and for further discussion about how or, in some cases, whether we should proceed. Where appropriate, this exercise also helps focus on relevant dates, such as statutes of limitations or other periods of time that ultimately should be docketed to ensure that they are not lost.

Finally, I utilize the scope of work to estimate the total fees and costs. I always note that the bottom line is, in fact, just an estimate (indeed, at times I include a range of numbers) with the actual fees and costs being based upon the amount of time expended and actual costs. I also note that if I anticipate fees exceed greatly my estimate, I will provide that information to the client as early as possible so a decision can be made on how to proceed.

Once this is written into the retention agreement, I discuss it with the client. Execution of the agreement serves to at least partially ensure that the client is not surprised about the way representation proceeds and with the fees and costs that are incurred. (I have included a sample scope of work outline in Appendix D.)

Conflicts

Of course, while certain conflicts or appearance of conflicts preclude any representation, other issues that I lump within the area of "conflicts" may not. These might, for example, include issue-related conflicts or conflicts associated with the concepts of "sides" in environmental law. The bulk of my practice involves the representation of public and private clients who are faced with the need to navigate through the regulatory process or who are involved in some litigation over their actions or inactions. This could be contrasted with the role of a lawyer who routinely takes a plaintiff's position in cost-recovery and clean-up actions or those who represent environmental groups or interests who are advocating some kind of general or specific environmental protection. In this type of practice it is difficult to change sides and move from the defense to the plaintiff's side in cases involving legal or factual issues that are the same or similar to ones you are likely to confront when representing a defendant. Even if no direct client conflict exists, at best the new representation is awkward and, in most cases, existing clients or potential future clients simply do not understand and are not interested in any explanation of your motives. The best policy is one that simply avoids the problem by focusing on one side or the other.

Now having articulated the best policy, I must admit that at times I have represented clients with interests different from the interests I usually represent. For example, in representing one of my large public-agency clients, I filed suit against another public agency over a matter of significance to both of them. The crux of the lawsuit was to stop the other agency from taking an action that would cause environmental harm to areas within the boundaries of my client.

I recognized in undertaking the representation that I would need to take positions on certain issues that were contrary in general to the positions I had taken or might need to take on behalf of other clients. Moreover, the case was one that had a great deal of public exposure and there was no way that I could avoid, even if I desired to do so, other clients knowing about the litigation or my role in it.

In proceeding with the representation, I took a tack of full disclosure. I hid nothing about my representation. I noted that the public agency was a client of longstanding and that the position we asserted was consistent with the law. I told clients and potential clients that if they were uncomfortable with my representation of this public agency in the litigation, I would assist them in obtaining different legal counsel. The end result was that I lost no clients and I have never perceived a diminution in business because of that representation. Nonetheless, it is not a practice that I would recommend to others, nor is it a practice that could or should be maintained in anything other than limited circumstances.

I have also at times represented pro bono or otherwise an environmental "cause." Again, I am not certain that this is a good policy. However, when I have done it, I have proceeded carefully, ensuring first that no actual conflict of interest exists. I also engage in a course of full disclosure to the "environmental" client, noting that I can take no position adverse to the interests of an existing client. This also requires me to select the environmental cause fairly carefully, avoiding issues or likely issues of interest to my existing clients. I also routinely discuss the nature of this type of representation with my other clients. The full disclosure should be made within the attorney–client retention agreement.

The Ability to Terminate the Relationship

Sometimes the attorney–client relationship just does not work. The client, of course, has the right to terminate the relationship at any time with or without cause. I believe that the lawyer should, within ethical constraints, retain a similar ability and, as a consequence, like to draft a provision to this effect into the retention agreement. This provision should explain the process for terminating the relationship and explain how billings are to be dealt with, as well as how transfer of files and other relevant relationship issues are to be dealt with. This provision should be fairly expressed and not leave very much for discussion at that point when the relationship terminates. As a practical matter, the ability to "fire" a client may be as crucial to the success of a practice as the ability to obtain and retain clients.

Other Client Intake Related Matters

The attorney–client retention agreement is a crucial element of client intake. Unless some other arrangement has been made, I do not consider the attorney–client relationship to have started until it is executed. However, other aspects of client intake other than the retention agreement need to be considered.

Who undertakes the initial discussion with the client depends in large part on how the client first contacts the firm. That first contact, however, should identify the broad issues involved and attempt to elicit, as best as possible, enough information to run an initial conflict-of-interest check. This usually includes the names of all relevant parties on all sides of the issue, as well as aliases and enough description to be able to, in general terms, describe the nature of the proposed representation. I also like to determine how or why the firm was contacted. This allows you to provide appropriate credit for business development.

The intaking lawyer then needs to assess the situation and determine whether the firm can, in fact, deal with the matter presented and, if so, who should be assigned. Once this is done and an initial conflict check completed, then a meeting can be confirmed with the potential client.

I like to minimize the number of lawyers present at the initial client meeting. Even though a number of lawyers may be involved in representing the client's interests, they do not all necessarily need to be present at the same time. (I do, however, go out of my way to introduce the client to other lawyers as early as possible.) During the initial meeting, the client needs to be allowed to provide you with as much information as possible and whatever documents available that are relevant to the case. During this initial meeting I also determine if a site visit is needed and whether a full initial assessment will require meeting with others, for example, staff at a regulatory agency. During this meeting I take notes that become the basis of the scope of work that I prepare as part of the attorney–client retention agreement.

Based upon this initial meeting, I determine if I am willing to undertake representation. If I am, I make arrangements for the next phase of work, including the completion of a more detailed and final conflict check, and the completion of the attorney–client retention agreement. I also discuss at that time billing and other related arrangements as well as a retainer if appropriate in any given situation.

I should note that at times this entire intake process is compressed and most everything takes place at one time, or close to it. Indeed, depending upon the situation—including urgency and scope—it can all happen on the telephone. However, in the end, two things should have been completed. First, the conflict check must have been completed with confirmation that no conflicts of interest exist; and second, an attorney–client retention agreement, including a scope of work, should have been executed.

It is, however, the case that in some circumstances the establishment of the attorney–client relationship is not quite as clear-cut or neat as you would like it to be. I cannot even begin to count the times that a client has come to me with an "emergency" situation in which some action, on my part, is needed immediately. In these situations, it may, as an ethical matter, be that the attorney–client relationship starts much earlier than the establishment of a "business" relationship through the execution of the formal retention agreement. Nonetheless, even in these situations, I am fairly clear about what is expected or should be expected on both sides of the relationship, including expectations with respect to timing related to the issuance of legal opinions or the preparation and filing of litigation-related documents. I am also clear with respect to anticipated fees and costs.

In these situations, I also ensure, to the extent possible, that no conflicts of interest exist. I undertake this check based upon a first review of the matter and of the parties and issues that will likely be involved. I check this information against my knowledge as well as against the firm's client list. Assuming that no apparent conflict is uncovered, I proceed with the representation, subject to completion of our more formal conflict-of-interest review. I have, on rare occasions, had to withdraw from the representation of a client because of later-discovered conflicts. I have as a rule disclosed the conflict to the existing client and have, in some situations, refunded or refused fees that otherwise would have been appropriate.

Once you are retained, there needs to be consideration given to implementation of the scope of work. This requires two specific actions. The first requires that lawyers be assigned with some clear understanding of what work is to be undertaken by whom and how supervision is to proceed. The second is to docket key dates that are mandated by some external requirements, such as an applicable statute of limitations. In addition, internal dates tied to the scope of work timeline should also be docketed. Support staff should be charged with continually updating these docket sheets based upon lawyer input, and both staff and lawyers should be responsible for reviewing docketed information and conforming to the timelines. In addition, one lawyer, or particularly in larger firms a legal assistant or paralegal, not necessarily involved with the client or the work at issue, should be assigned the overall task of checking with lawyers as dates noted within the docket approach.

I should add, at this point, that in the context of docketing, as well as other client intake and caseload-management matters, there are any number of outstanding software programs that can be utilized to assist. I know this because I have bought and used almost all of them. In the end, however, these systems are only as effective as you are in utilizing them. Effectiveness in utilizing these systems requires regularity in use. You need to integrate these systems into your daily routine or they will not work. You also must have the time to keep them up to date and, of course, the time to actively undertake the actual legal work that is the subject of your management system. This requires real time management and an ability or resolve not to overcommit your time, neither of which I have been overly successful in accomplishing in my own practice. At times the best I can manage is the preparation of hand-written "to-do" lists as a means of ensuring that important dates are not missed.

Alternative Forms of Agreement

It is not uncommon when retained by a large corporate entity or by a public agency to be presented with a form attorney–client retention agreement prepared by the client's in-house legal counsel. I have no inherent problem with executing these agreements as an alternative to the one that I prepare. I do, however, read them carefully and make appropriate modifications. I also seek to amend them, if necessary, to incorporate or cover the various issues that I have otherwise discussed here. In particular, either as an appendix, or as a separate document, I like to include some variant of the scope of work.

Billing

A successful firm needs to consider cash flow and, as a consequence, the capabilities of clients to pay and pay on time. This is the part that I find the hardest to deal with. I like to practice law; I do not necessarily like to be a businessman. Nonetheless, I remind myself that a law practice is a business and, as a consequence, payment is essential.

Billing should follow consistently with what is written within the attorney–client retention agreement. There are three types of basic billing arrangements that might be utilized as part of the environmental law practice: (1) hourly billing; (2) contingent fee billing; and (3) citizen suit/attorneys. In addition, there are any number of variables from these basic arrangements that might be relevant.

Hourly Billing Arrangements

The hourly billing arrangement is one in which services are rendered for a set hourly rate, with rates assigned to each lawyer based upon experience, skill, and firm economics, and rates also assigned for legal assistants, secretarial, and law clerk time, as appropriate. Rates are included within the agreement and the ability to raise rates, as appropriate, is also provided for.

Time is recorded in increments. I use increments of six minutes, dividing an hour into ten parts. I record my time on worksheets that are in the form of daily calendars developed through a computer program, with scheduled appointments already recorded by my secretary. I then annotate this calendar throughout the day with details and specific time notations. I have found that a failure to provide this detail creates a situation where it is impossible to accurately recreate a day's work. The net result is that, when this has occurred, I have erred on the side of the client and have underbilled, thereby losing time and revenue to my economic detriment. As a consequence, I stress the need to carefully record time.

I then periodically transfer this time to daily summary sheets. At this point I amplify the discussion of the work I have undertaken and adjust time billed, as appropriate. I use this time to ensure that I have not underbilled or overbilled a client. This sheet is then entered into the computer billing program by my secretary.

The billing program that we use allows you to open up a client account from your computer, enter the nature of the work undertaken, and to set a timer that will automatically record time. This desktop program is then linked to the billing program. This reduces all of the paper steps I have noted above into one step. I do not use this program for a number of reasons. The two most significant are that I travel a lot and need to be able to record my time away from the office, and my general aversion to overreliance on computers. I am working hard on overcoming this latter problem and a laptop could, of course, deal with the former.

The hourly billing arrangement also requires clients to cover costs. Costs are of two types: ordinary and extraordinary.

Ordinary costs include normal overhead, including secretarial time, copying costs, telephone, and similar matters. Three means exist to deal with these costs. First, you can itemize these costs and bill them pro rata. This is time-consuming and not a very efficient way to proceed. Second, you can assume a flat "administrative fee." This is a satisfactory means of covering these costs, but some clients do not like the apparent arbitrary nature of the fee. Third, these costs can be reflected and covered within the hourly rates. This, of course, internalizes these costs and avoids conflicts with clients.

Extraordinary costs include conference telephone calls, the costs associated with travel, large copying costs, court or other filings, overnight-mail costs, meals, deposition costs, costs of expert witnesses. These costs should be itemized and documented and included with the client's bill.

Bills should be generated on a monthly basis with payment expected within 30 days of billing. That should be made clear to the client. Cash flow is an important factor in firm success. If bills are not paid on time, the firm will need to borrow money in order to continue operation. The cost of borrowing money then becomes an additional cost of operation. I add an interest component, noted in the attorney–client retention agreement, for bills that are in excess of 30 days late. (I, of course, review this policy carefully and balance its use against overall client relationships and the reason for the late payments. I do not always assess the interest rate even though technically I could.)

Bills should be carefully reviewed to ensure that they are accurate and that they contain enough detail for the client to understand what has been done. I do not consider a total billed figure with an explanation of "for services rendered" sufficient. I believe that detail avoids conflict with clients about billing practices.

Finally, in this regard, you need to take action immediately if past due bills start to grow. And the time to act to avoid economic harm to your practice may not be very long. In some cases, being 60 days overdue is much too long. As noted earlier, an environmental practice is time intensive and bills can grow quickly for any one client. You simply cannot afford to continue to work for clients who do not pay. This should be made clear to the client, and you must be prepared to take appropriate action to withdraw from representation if payments are not made.

Contingent Fee Arrangements

Contingent fee arrangements are most common in a litigation setting but can be utilized in other situations. Here, lawyers are compensated based upon an agreed-upon percentage of a recovery gained in litigation or a sum obtained in some other transaction. For the most part, subject to some statutory limitations, the terms are subject to negotiation.

With the exception of condemnation actions and, of course, toxic and hazardous tort actions, I generally do not like to enter into contingent fee arrangements. The practice of environmental law is just too time consuming to justify proceeding, in most cases, in this manner. When I do proceed in this manner, I like to have the client bear all or most of the responsibility for extraordinary costs. Even when my work is on a contingent fee basis, I record my time as if I am working on an hourly basis and I generate bills in the same manner. Depending upon the arrangements I have made with the client, I either hold these bills or provide them to the client for information. Should the attorney–client relationship terminate early, my fee arrangement usually provides that I be compensated on a "reasonable basis." I consider these bills and my normal rates as a beginning point for this part of the discussion. Additionally, in situations where attorneys' fees can be recovered, these types of billings are essential to justify a recovery.

Attorneys' Fee Awards

As noted earlier, many environmental statutes include citizen-suit provisions with attorneys' fee-shifting provisions if the plaintiff prevails. For the most part, how a lawyer handles billing in the interim is a matter of negotiation with the client. Various arrangements are possible, from payment of a small flat fee periodically as augmented upon success, to a reduced hourly rate agreement. Coverage of costs is similarly diverse with costs covered by clients in some instances and lawyers in others. The basic concept, however, is that the lawyer will be rewarded or the client reimbursed based upon the attorney fee award at the end. Since this award is often at the discretion of the court with the other side able to challenge the award, it is important to keep detailed billing records. Again, the hourly billing model is the best way to do this with daily records kept to support the ultimate bill.

Variations on Billing Themes

At various times, I have been asked and have, in fact, considered and adopted alternative billing arrangements. These requests have normally been made by a large corporate entity that offers a great deal of work and that is shopping around among a great number of eager law firms or in some instances by a public agency for whom I have done a lot of work. I have a mixed view about these types of arrangements. The reason for this mixed view is fairly simple to state: You would assume that billing rates have been reasonably established based upon some type of economic decision making specific to your firm. If this is the case, firm economics dictate that you obtain a given number of dollars for each hour that is worked. As a consequence, any "alternative" billing arrangement must take this into consideration. An alternative billing consideration that does not return this equivalent over a billing period means that the law firm is injured in some material way. An alternative billing arrangement that brings in more dollars during this period obviously is not to the advantage of the client.

In spite of what is probably my preference for a standard hourly billing rate, I have, on occasion, offered and utilized alternative billing arrangements. The one I am most attracted to is a blended or melded rate. In this model, I first determine which lawyers are likely to work on the project and the amount of time that each might spend. From this information I develop a flat rate that I offer to the client for all work undertaken by the firm. An example of how this would work follows.

Assume two lawyers work on the case, one who bills at $130 per hour and another who bills at $225 per hour. Further assume that the $130 per hour lawyer will work three hours for each one hour the higher-billing lawyer works. Utilizing this 3:1 ratio as a basis for developing the blended rate ((3 x $130 per hour) + (1 x $225 per hour)/4), the firm's rate would be about $155 per hour. Assuming the lawyers work consistent with that ratio billing is, of course, about what it would be on a normal rate basis. However, shifts in assignments with the higher-billing lawyer working more hours than what were estimated results in a lower effective rate to the client. More hours worked by the lower-billing lawyer than what were estimated will result in higher fees. The end result will also be influenced by the number of hours lawyers with varying billing rates, in the middle of the range, bill for work for the project.

The bottom line is that while some risk does exist that billing will be either higher or lower than normal billing rates, a goal of leveling the rate schedule does occur.

Another means to address this issue is, of course, to undertake work based upon a flat retainer. Under this practice, a firm would undertake work for a client based upon a flat monthly rate, regardless of the number of hours actually worked. This flat monthly rate would be negotiated with possible adjustments to reflect economic reality over time. There is no reason why this type of billing arrangement cannot work, particularly if the retainer is first established in a rational manner.

Still another means of proceeding is to develop different rates for different types of clients based upon objective criteria. For example, I use a dual rate schedule that bills public agency clients at a lower rate than private clients. I do this for a number of reasons.

First, public agency work is both interesting and rewarding. I like to do it and, as a consequence, encourage public agency clients to retain us by offering lower rates than those I charge others.

Second, public agencies pay and, in most situations, pay promptly. Cash flow is important and it alone can justify a lower rate. In contrast, over the years some private clients have been very slow in paying and, in addition, some have simply not paid me at all. The costs of these disappointing transactions have justified the higher rates for private clients.

Third, public agency work tends to be intense. In other words, there is a lot of it. As a consequence, the volume of work provided by clients who pay and pay on time justifies economically lower rates.

This last point is worth underscoring and, indeed, justifies still another variation on the billing theme and explains, at least to a degree, why I am not entirely adverse to developing a special rate, for any client, in certain situations where I know that there will be a volume of work and where the client will pay and pay on time. The actual rate involved can be suggested by either you or the client and negotiated until both are satisfied.

Three points of some importance should be noted as part of this discussion.

1. You need to make certain that you provide an opportunity to review and, upon providing reasonable notice, adjust rates from time to time. An adjustment in rates can reflect a whole host of issues from inflation to increased over-head. Regardless of the reason, there is nothing worse than finding yourself in a situation where you are working hours and hours on behalf of a client and are, nonetheless, losing money. No one is well served in this type of situation. Being honest about the fact that rates will be reviewed and perhaps adjusted, over time, will avoid numerous potential future problems.

2. You need to consider that negotiation and transactional work may result in litigation. What was a reasonable rate for transactional work may not be sufficient to support the type of time commitment that is needed in litigation. Any special fee agreement should include a provision noting that rates may need to be adjusted if the matter results in litigation.

3. Finally, alternative billing arrangements make billing and accounting more difficult. As you develop these rates you need to keep this practical concern in mind. Monthly billing that includes different billing rates or billing arrangements for each client may create an administrative

nightmare that overcomes the desire to accommodate clients' needs.

Regardless of what rate-setting structure is employed, it must reflect an overall cost structure that both meets the firm's as well as the client's needs. To facilitate this, the type of scope of work presentation I discussed earlier is prepared and discussed with the client. As you recall, among other things, this scope of work identifies who will do what, with an eye to providing services in the most efficient and cost-effective manner possible. Additionally, providing the best service at the most reasonable rates requires the lawyer to provide estimates and targets that can on an ongoing basis be discussed and reviewed with the client, and work adjusted based upon these economic considerations. Finally, providing clients with clear, accurate, and reasonably detailed descriptions of the work undertaken with the corresponding number of hours that were involved allows the client an opportunity to monitor and discuss the appropriateness of bills with his lawyers. This way of proceeding may not be all that creative, but I know that it works. I just do not think that there are any shortcuts.

In this regard, one large "variation" on billing alternatives (assuming you can call it a "variation" instead of a "world of its own") is what insurance companies want to do. What they want to do is to pay as little as possible and, in the process, to create as much additional administrative hassle, with its consequential costs, as they can. I do not work with insurance companies, as a rule. When I do, I do not adjust my rates and I will only modify "administrative" practices to the extent that what is proposed can be done in a reasonable fashion. Proceeding in any other fashion (unless your practice is one that is specifically geared to working with insurance carriers) simply is not cost-effective, nor is it calculated to enhance your enjoyment of the practice of environmental law.

Space

An environmental law practice is paper intensive. I have, on countless occasions, had one or two small matters to take care of over the weekend. Rather than returning to the office to do the work, I have chosen to take the work home. However, rather than being able to take the work home in a small binder or in my briefcase, I have had to load boxes of documents, reports, regulations, and like materials into my car in order to be able to address a more or less simple piece of work. This is simply one of the facts of life associated with an environmental law practice. There is a lot of paper.

The consequence of this more or less unique aspect of environmental law to law-office management is that adequate space is critical. File rooms, libraries, and office space devoted, all or in part, to a single case or client is not unusual. The law office simply must be able to accommodate the in-house storage of extensive materials.

Storage space also needs to be flexible enough to accommodate various means of storing material. Space needs to be planned, of course, to accommodate more traditional files in the classic file-room model. However, in addition, there needs to be some ability to store client- or matter-specific materials in a manner similar to library storage where technical materials can be easily seen and retrieved. Similarly, this type of space should be made available for the storage of binders that may contain thousands of documents that need to be retrievable and reviewable in a similar manner. Finally, storage space must be planned for boxes of materials relevant to an active case or to the ongoing representation of a client.

In addition to these storage space questions, but directly related, is the need to have some active work space within these storage areas. It is not efficient when reviewing these materials to continually remove them to your office or alternative work area. Having tables or work stations within these storage areas maximizes the efficiency by which you can proceed.

I believe that the amount of storage space needed within the law-firm layout is disproportionate to what the ratio would be in firms with other types of practices. Do not underestimate the need for storage space as you undertake your law-office space planning.

No matter how well you plan, you simply will not be able to store all of your client files and materials on-site. As a consequence, in addition to in-house storage capability, the firm needs to be able to also store materials off-site. There are a number of ways to do this, ranging from the rental of self-maintained storage space to the utilization of storage services. These storage services provide the advantage of being able to call for pick-up or delivery of materials and includes insurance, safety, and security assurances.

As part of your space planning, you will need to decide what files and materials can be stored off-site. This again requires some advance planning and discipline in carrying through with the plan. Additionally, materials sent for off-site storage should be completely and accurately indexed so that efficiency in the retrieval of stored files is maximized.

This last point is, of course, not unique to files stored off-site. Files stored in-house also should be completely and accurately indexed to maximize the efficiency of retrieval. There is nothing more frustrating than to view the extensive files and materials generated in an environmental law practice and not be able to quickly retrieve what is needed.

Now, everything that I have noted with respect to storage space, in theory, should be affected by the advances in law-office technology that provides for the storage of an incredible amount of material within the confines of a desktop or laptop computer or within a single compact disk. Indeed, to some degree it is. The problem in relying entirely on these alternatives, as I have observed it, presents itself in two ways.

First, we are still in a transition period. Most firms currently have a great deal of paper material that needs to be stored now, and transforming this paper into an electronic form is just too costly and time-consuming to be feasible. As a consequence, existing paper requires that you be concerned about the adequacy of storage space. Additionally, a lot of the paper is generated by third parties who do not have the capability or the desire to provide materials in any other form. This may be the case, in particular, with significant and relevant technical or other background materials and is certainly the case with respect to routine correspondence.

Second, even in those situations where most of the paper is or can be transferred, reasons exist to continue to also have these same materials available in paper form. This second reason may be a relic of the fact that not everyone is comfortable with these types of technologies, or that the generation of paper, in this regard, is simply unavoidable. Nonetheless, parallel means of storage need to be accommodated.

Your Library

The proper size and extent of an environmental library involves many of the same considerations noted above. In addition to needing the basics of any general law library, the environmental law library needs to include treatises dealing with specific substantive areas of the law, desk books focused on environmental practice areas, newsletter information dealing with the current state of the law, as well as access to federal, state, and local ordinances and regulations that are associated with specific practice areas. Additionally, environmental law libraries often contain technical manuals or treatises dealing with technical areas associated with the practice of environmental law, such as engineering, toxicity, chemistry, biology, or other technical fields.

The environmental law library is as much, if not more, affected by advances in technology than what was discussed with respect to storage space. Almost all general legal materials are available electronically. You can either subscribe to a research service and access these materials through the telephone, or you can purchase these materials on compact disk. How you proceed depends, in large part, on how the law firm is situated. Nonetheless, as discussed later in the context of "technology," the need to be properly equipped with the capability to access and utilize these electronic sources is essential.

Technology

For the most part, the technological needs of an environmental practice are the same as those within any law firm. However, there are additional reasons why electronic technologies need to be adopted sooner rather than later within an environmental law practice. As noted earlier, storage space and library space needed for an environmental practice is extensive. Adoption of alternative means to house and store these materials will serve to reduce the space and consequent expense associated with these items. They may also make retrieval of these materials and resources more efficient. The interface with other technologies also serves to heighten the need to be able to work in the large world that is also relevant to an environmental law practice. Remember, a great deal of what an environmental law practice deals with is information that is generated by third parties, including regulatory agencies. These agencies have shifted to technology and, as a consequence, so must the environmental lawyer. The following are but a few of the technologies that should be considered as part of the environmental law office.

Personal Computers

Every lawyer must have either a desktop or laptop personal computer. They have become essential to the practice of environmental law. Not only are they needed for all of the general purposes that are associated with the practice of any type of law, but there are unique reasons that they are particularly useful in the practice of environmental law.

First, personal computers allow you to access the stored material and library material discussed above, thus allowing the better integration of the individual lawyer's efforts into space planning and other management considerations.

Second, they allow the lawyer to access technical materials that are being produced on compact disk. It is not at all uncommon for relevant regulatory agencies to make proposed rules or draft environmental documents or other important technical materials available on compact disk. The environmental lawyer must be able to access these materials.

Third, PCs allow access to the Internet. The Internet has become an essential extension of the lawyer's law library. Almost all local, state, and federal agencies relevant to the practice of environmental law have web sites. These agencies routinely post their latest informational findings, rules, regulations, decisions, and other relevant materials there. In order to practice and compete, the environmental lawyer needs to have easy access to these places.

Additionally, business and technical associations and businesses that form the client base for an environmental law practice also have web sites. In order to be competitive the environmental lawyer must have the ability to also easily access these sites.

Fourth, computers allow communication with regulatory agencies, clients, and others through e-mail. This can include more or less routine communications or the transmission of working documents in a fast, efficient manner. Recently I worked with clients and technical experts, spread across various states, on the development of a response to comments on a technical environmental document we had generated. The base document had been transmitted to all by e-mail, which I had displayed on my computer screen while I spoke to the others through the telephone software that also was being run by my computer.

Scanners

The use of scanners is not unique to the environmental law practice. However, with the amount of paper that is generated and will need to be stored, it is never too early to start to transfer hard copies into computer files for storage and easy access. Current scanner and OCR programs work and are a cost-effective means of beginning this process.

Copy Machines

Like the use of scanners, copy machine utilization is not unique to the environmental law practice. Nonetheless, this type of practice requires the generation of a great deal of paper and the need to duplicate a lot of it. Exactly how you proceed depends in large part on the size of the practice involved. The economics of a large firm may justify the capital costs of equipment and the in-house reproduction of most of what is needed. Mid-sized or smaller firm economics, on the other hand, may justify sending most copying jobs out of house. Nonetheless, some in-house capability is necessary. Modern digital copiers offer the ability to combine scanning technology with copying technology and also avoid some of the more mechanical failures that otherwise occupy and waste a great deal of support staff time. They are, of course, more expensive than other types of copiers. These relative costs need to be evaluated.

Support Staff

The support staff employed in any law firm depends in significant part on the size of the firm. Where the large firm may employ legal secretaries, word processors, receptionists, operators, administrators, bookkeepers, accountants, clerks who copy materials, process mail and undertake filing, messengers, legal assistants, law school interns and clerks, and people who serve a whole host of other in-house functions, a small firm may only employ a legal secretary. There is nothing unique to the practice of environmental law that would necessarily dictate the extent of support staff that should be hired.

Moreover, a significant amount of what support staff undertakes as part of their job is a matter of personal preference and relates to the type of working relationship that has been established. For example, my secretary and I have worked together for more than fourteen years and I rely upon her to, among other things, communicate directly with clients, oversee my schedule, and screen my telephone calls, in addition to the production of a range of documents including letters, contracts, legal briefs, and comments on technical materials. In short, my secretary plays an indispensable role in the success of my law practice. Other lawyers may not feel comfortable placing this type of reliance in their secretary.

To the extent that there is anything unique with respect to support staff in the context of an environmental law practice, it revolves around the fact that just like the environmental lawyer, everyone who works within an environmental law practice needs to have some training that is specific to the needs of that practice. They must understand and be able to deal with the unique issues associated with environmental law in order to maximize the competence and efficiency of the representation that is to be provided.

This, of course, includes training in the unique substantive and procedural aspects of environmental law.

Stated another way, I view support staff, my secretary, legal assistant, and file-room assistant as competent professionals capable of doing their jobs. This means that I rely upon them to do the job that they have been hired to do. Accordingly, for example, I expect files (both normal as well as the ongoing and extensive working files that I discussed earlier) to be kept in proper order and to be kept in such a way as to make efficient and timely retrieval possible. This requires not only knowledge about the client, the matters involved, and the contents of files, but also coordination among my secretary, legal assistant, and file-room assistant.

In this context, because my secretary has direct contact with clients, she must have a basic knowledge not only of specific issues of concern to the client, but also some understanding of the underlying legal context from which these specific issues derive.

Ensuring that your legal assistant is well grounded in the areas of environmental law in which you practice is also of critical importance. Having a legal assistant who is familiar with the processes and personnel at relevant regulatory agencies, for example, expands your ability to maintain routine contact with those agencies. It also allows routine matters, such as the review of agency files, to be undertaken without your personal attention. Additionally, the organization of the extensive paper and computer-related materials associated with this practice can be very efficiently managed by a competently trained legal assistant with specialized environmental legal knowledge.

Continuing Legal Education

As noted earlier, modern environmental law is no more than thirty to forty years old. During that fairly short period of time the law has grown through the enactment of numerous statutory provisions and ordinances and the promulgation of countless rules and regulations; and the issuance of an array of administrative agency and judicial decisions. Moreover, this has occurred at the federal, state, and local level. On top of all of this, because the area of the law is so young, it is very dynamic, continuing to grow at alarming rates. All of this poses a truly daunting task to the environmental lawyer. You simply must keep abreast of all of this. You must keep current. Doing so will require you to account for the time and expense of continued legal education. You will also need to consider keeping up with the technical side of environmental law, which will require additional time and expense.

There are, of course, numerous courses offered in almost every practice area. The key, in some respects, is to be careful in the process of selection so you maximize what you obtain for the time and money you expend. The best way to maximize success in this regard is to check with others. Word of mouth tends to be the most certain road to satisfaction.

In looking at possible courses, you should also consider the availability of written materials as well as audio or video tapes. These alternative means of acquiring new information may be cost-effective and less time consuming than other options.

The Business Aspects of the Environmental Law Practice

One final point of note. There is clearly a distinct difference between having a successful environmental law practice and having a successful law business. You can have a thriving practice dealing with all of the intricacies of environmental law with numerous good clients and still not have a successful business. The two are not the same and the attributes that lead to success in one may not be the same type of things that will lead to success in the other.

This book is primarily about developing a successful environmental law practice, not on how to operate a successful business. Nonetheless, like most everything, there are areas of overlap which, where appropriate (particularly in this chapter), I have noted. In addition, the following, very general, concepts should be kept in mind:

♦ The first is fairly obvious: keep in mind that your practice is, in fact, a business. Not only do you depend upon it for a living, but so do those who work for and with you. As a consequence, you need to focus on the economic return associated with the work you undertake as well as the economic consequences of your actions. If the money-side of things, for whatever reason, offends your notion of "professionalism," keep in mind that if you are not in business you will not be able to apply your professional skills to resolve interesting and crucial problems.

♦ An environmental law firm needs to have a "business person." Whether the role is undertaken full or part time by a lawyer or nonlawyer depends upon the given situation and personal preference. Nonetheless, someone must have the primary role of looking after the business part of the practice. All lawyers need to be aware of the business side of the practice, even if they are not directly involved.

♦ Everyone needs to carry their own weight. I can think of nothing more destructive than situations in which a lawyer or lawyers are simply not working at a level sufficient to pay their own way. This does not mean that there can be no time for associates to learn the profession or for others to develop their practice. However, in general, and over time, each member of a firm must contribute. Other lawyers should not feel as if they are "carrying" others.

♦ Lawyers who bring in business or who bill a great number of hours need to be fairly compensated, and must also feel as if they have a real voice in how the firm is managed and in decision making. The exact form that this takes will vary from firm to firm depending upon size and preferences. Nonetheless, leveraged lawyers need to feel invested in the economics and management of the firm.

♦ A firm needs to develop a personality and then attempt to socialize its associates and members to this way of life. Again, firm personality can vary in any number of ways and, indeed, one firm's personality can be the opposite of another's. The point, however, is that whatever that personality is, it needs to be understood and then passed on to others in the firm.

♦ A firm needs to watch its associates to ensure that they are developing as high-quality lawyers and that they are adhering to the business and practice procedures developed by the firm. The more successful the firm (and more busy its members), the more crucial this point becomes.

♦ A firm needs to watch its members (including its most senior partners) to ensure that they continue to develop as high-quality lawyers and maintain their already high level of lawyering, and that they continue to adhere to the business and practice procedures developed by the firm. Again, the more successful the firm (and more busy its members), the more crucial this point becomes.

♦ A firm needs to continue to be sensitive to interpersonal relationships among lawyers and staff. Lawyers need to be responsive to problems and dissatisfaction and know when to take action and when to refrain from doing so.

Obtaining and Keeping Clients 6

THERE ARE, OF COURSE, NUMEROUS TREATISES and articles focused on the task of obtaining clients. These resources, in general terms, describe advertising options, memberships in social organizations, lawyer referral services, and a whole host of other means of obtaining clients. Some of these sound reasonable to me and I have no reason to doubt that they can be adopted and utilized by the environmental lawyer to develop a practice.

There are some unique aspects of obtaining clients in the environmental law practice that should be considered as part of the mix that you use in getting started.

I began my legal practice as a lawyer with the U.S. Department of the Interior. Later I served as an Assistant U.S. Attorney and a trial lawyer with the U.S. Department of Justice. I entered private practice with a great deal of experience and expertise, but with no clients. I spent the first six months of private practice working on odds and ends provided to me by others within the law firm I had joined and wondering whether I had made a big mistake leaving a government practice I enjoyed and where I had a great deal of autonomy for a private practice in which I was dependent on others for work.

From that time I have built a fairly extensive natural resources and environmental law practice that provides a substantial amount of work for fifteen lawyers, all of whom specialize in some facet or facets of environmental law. Getting here did not happen by chance.

When I understood that I needed to develop my own clients and practice to be happy in the private sector, I embarked upon the implementation of a plan that I hoped would within six months (the completion of my first full year in private practice) provide me with a self-sustaining client base. At the heart of the plan were the following concepts:

1. I wanted to create a focus to the practice upon which I could build. In this regard, I had in mind developing a practice that I would enjoy. I knew that in order to be successful I would need to hone my expertise in the substantive and procedural areas of the law in which I was involved. This type of focus, among other things, allowed me to identify target clients and client groups that would best benefit from the type of focused expertise that I wanted to offer.

2. As part of the development of a focused expertise, I made time to research and write on topics that were at the heart of the subject of my practice. My intention was to publish the results. I had two types of publications in mind. The first was a more technical, legal publication that would be read by other lawyers. Because the practice of environmental law is in itself specialized, other lawyers are a prime source of referrals. These lawyers either have a general practice and have identified the need for outside assistance, or they are themselves environmental lawyers but have identified the need to obtain more focused assistance in order to fully represent their clients. If these lawyers believe you to be expert, they will seek you out either for assistance or to refer a client to.

   The second type of publication I had in mind was one that targeted more directly the underlying client base that

I had identified. This type of publication is less technical and geared to the lay audience.

3. I next identified professional legal associations relevant to the areas of environmental law in which I wanted to focus and then I joined them. Again, referral from other lawyers is fertile ground for client development and, as a consequence, meeting these other lawyers is important.

4. I also identified professional associations to which my target client base belonged. I joined these associations and became active in their legal-affairs group. These types of contacts are crucial for the development of business. Attending conferences offered by these associations also allows you to better understand the type of real problems that confront the people and businesses that you represent. It also allows you an opportunity to interact with clients in a manner that is not otherwise available.

5. I identified professional associations in which other environmental professionals were involved. As I will discuss later, engineers, biologists, toxicologists, and professionals in other fields related to your environmental practice can provide you with many client referrals.

6. I arranged to make formal presentations and to speak to each of the groups that I identified above. This provided me with broad exposure and helped identify me as someone who is competent and expert in the areas of my focus. Talks to client groups, as opposed to professional groups, should focus on practical issues and problems rather than the more esoteric and remote. Being able to offer yourself as an expert on a matter of practical importance to a potential client is far better than receiving a great deal of academic acclaim for a speech you have given or an article you have written.

7. Over the years I have advertised only to a limited degree. Where I have done this I have limited the effort to publications or association newsletters that cater to associations and client groups where clients are likely to be obtained. On occasion I have also sponsored events at an associa-

tion conference. These types of focused advertising tend
to serve to place your name in front of other lawyers and
clients in the context of your expertise.

8. In the past, firms I have been a part of have published
    newsletters that have been distributed to existing clients
    and a potential client base. While this can be a great deal
    of work, I believe that it is prudent to consider the publi-
    cation of a specialized newsletter or participation as a con-
    tributor to an existing newsletter as part of the client-
    development effort. Again, this will not only allow you to
    further your substantive knowledge in the area you write
    about, but also further your general exposure within your
    targeted client community.

9. Once I established a client base, I found that the best way
    to develop additional clients was through word of mouth
    and referrals from my existing client base. Keep in mind
    that a solid environmental law practice is built over time.
    In this regard, each existing client should be viewed not
    only as a source of additional work in and of itself, but also
    as a source of potential future referrals.

10. Assuming that your practice is a part of, or is being devel-
    oped as an addition to, an existing more general practice,
    you should first identify clients within that existing client
    base that might best be aided by the focus that you have
    developed. Once identified, have lawyers who are current-
    ly in contact with the client introduce you. As an alterna-
    tive (or in addition) announcements and other types of
    notices circulated to clients should emphasize the initia-
    tion of the environmental law practice. If the firm already
    circulates a firm newsletter, you should publish an article
    that introduces the practice and perhaps provide some
    general information of practical use to the client.

11. As part of any marketing program firms should develop
    brochure-type materials that describe the firm and its
    practice, as well as individual lawyers and their back-
    ground and experience. You can get as fancy as you like in
    creating these materials. Options run from professionally
    done glossy brochures with a lot of pictures to profession-

al-looking materials created on firm letterhead. In all cases, however, the basics are the same: you will want the materials to explain fully the nature of the practice; the firm's ability to compete within the legal market; and to fully describe the lawyers within the firm.

   I like to keep all of this very simple and to the point. I have opted for the less formal brochure type that can be modified within the office to meet the exact situation for which the materials are intended. I even have long-form and short-form "biographies" that I can use depending on the situation in which I want to use the materials (see Appendices E and F for sample biographies).

12.   Another area where I tend to use more professionally prepared materials is where we want to make announcements of new lawyers or the transition of an associate to partner or shareholder status. This allows us to provide a mailing to all of our past and existing clients as well as to an additional diverse mailing list, which has been developed over time.

13.   Finally, in this regard, is the more formal proposal letter that is often requested by potential clients. This letter is tailored to address the specific situation for which it is intended. The letter proposal can be as formal and professionally done as you feel comfortable. Again, I prefer the less formal approach. In any event, the proposal letter can follow a more or less constant format that includes general information on the firm and its lawyers and should include brochure and biographical materials (see Appendices E and F). I also include a list of clients and references in this type of letter and spend some time discussing the specifics of the potential work, providing information on how the work will be undertaken and who from the firm will be involved. I have enclosed a sample proposal letter in Appendix G.

   As part of the general consideration of creating a client-development plan, you need to consider the mix of clients that you want to target.

Private Sector Clients

There are, of course, almost an unlimited number of opportunities to develop work within the private sector. Indeed, the areas from which this type of client base can be developed are almost as extensive, if not more extensive, than the areas of possible environmental practice. Prospective private sector clients include: potential tort plaintiffs where individualized damages are alleged; real estate developers where toxic substances or leaking underground storage tanks are at issue; and those that own or run business that may have a specific potential for environmental concerns, such solvents used as part of a dry cleaners or air emissions associated with the baking of bread, but could involve such diverse interests as agriculture or silvaculture where specific environmental protections exist or where habitat modification is controlled by the ESA.

In addition to the potential broad-based private sector clients, you may choose to focus your initial marketing to more specialized private sector clients, such as larger corporate businesses with a potential for large-scale and volume business. Examples of this include oil companies, large real estate developers, and other businesses that do a lot of one thing that may be highly regulated or subject to regulation. The key, however, is to think through this large potential base of private sector clients and to target a finite group for initial contact.

Almost every aspect of life today is controlled or regulated based upon some kind of environmental concern. As a consequence, the potential for the development of an environmental practice is everywhere.

In this regard, knowing that there is a lot of client potential within the private sector is meaningless unless you can develop a strategy for converting this potential into an actual client base and work. The first step is to reduce the focus of your efforts to something that is manageable. This requires you to decide on what part or parts of the environmental law you are going to deal with and the exact nature of the practice you want. Once you do this, you need to next focus on the industries that are most susceptible to this type of environmental regulation.

As I noted earlier, businesses tend to divide themselves by trade, and each trade or industry has developed associations that attempt to represent the collective interests of its members. The attention of many of these associations has been drawn to environmental issues specific to the trade at issue. Identifying these associations and then proceeding (as noted above) allows you to reduce your effort to a manageable level. Moreover, it also provides you with a series of steps as you move from one association to another to either develop an ever larger client base or, if at first you do not succeed, the next focus for your marketing attention.

Public Sector Clients

There are a lot of potential clients in the public sector. As noted earlier, public agencies must comply with statutory and regulatory constraints in the same manner as those within the private sector. In some situations they have even more significant obligations with which they must comply. While some of this compliance work and associated litigation is handled in-house, much of it is handled by outside legal counsel. For the most part, in-house counsel are general counsel and need assistance with the types of technical and complex issues that are posed in the environmental setting. This is particularly true with respect to smaller special districts.

In addition to the fact that the public sector has the potential for client generation, the work is also interesting. After all, for the most part it is the public sector that is involved in operating water-treatment facilities, wastewater-treatment facilities, solid-waste disposal sites. and other utility-related services. In addition, local land-use planning decisions also implicate transportation and related issues that involve a whole host of additional environmental issues. All of these activities are highly regulated and require these agencies to retain and rely upon those expert in this area of the law.

Marketing to clients in the public sector is not too different from what I noted earlier. Indeed, my client-development plan applies to this type of marketing in a similar manner to the way it applies to the private sector. In addition to the trade associations noted above, you should consider outreach and involvement in associations of cities, counties, local communities, or special districts. These entities and their conferences add additional avenues for your marketing activities.

The Proper Mix of Clients—
Billing Considerations

There are a number of ways that you can look at the mix of clients in order to facilitate cash flow. This mix can include public agency clients as well as private sector clients, and private sector clients can be both large and small. As I noted earlier, for the most part, public agency clients pay and pay regularly. Private sector clients can be all over the place with some small clients being punctual and some large private sector clients paying very slowly, if at all. Over the years I have dealt with these realities of payments in a number of ways. I have, for example, offered reduced hourly rates to large volume public (and some private) clients who pay within thirty days of billing, and I have increased hourly rates to clients within classes (normally private clients) that have been chronically late in payment. I have also insisted on retainers from smaller private clients before we have embarked upon large time-intensive projects where bills can run very high in a fairly short period of time.

This last point is fairly critical. A lot of environmental law work is very time-intensive and fees and costs can run up very quickly. In this regard, it is important that you always sit down with clients and be honest and up-front with respect to your billing rates, the estimated cost of your services, and your expectations with respect to prompt and full payment. It is far better to have a client walk away as a result of your candor before you have undertaken the time and effort of representation, than to have the client act surprised or be otherwise unwilling to make payment to you after you have taken the time and effort of representation.

Of course, even after all of your efforts, you may find clients unwilling or unable to pay or to pay promptly. While each situation must be evaluated on its own merits, in the end there is only one way to deal with this problem, and that is to identify the problem or potential as early as possible and to end the relationship soon thereafter. Any other way of proceeding will just lead to complications and further problems in which you fund or finance your client's legal services to your absolute detriment.

Also, as noted earlier, at various times I have had clients, particularly large, private sector clients, ask that we develop creative billing practices that result in lower legal fees. In this context, I have created, along with corporate counsel for the respective private sector clients, countless alternative billing arrangements to meet the desired corporate goal. While I do not necessarily discourage you from doing so, in the end, however, I have concluded that these arrangements either work to the benefit of the law firm, in which case I do not understand why the client would want to adopt them, or they work to the benefit of the client, in which case I do not know why the law firm would be interested. The bottom line is that you need to make a profit and your hourly billing rates should be set accordingly. Any arrangement that reduces that rate will reduce your profits and reduce your incentive to undertake the work in question.

Keeping Clients

As with the art of obtaining clients, there may not be anything unique about maintaining the clients of an environmental practice. Nonetheless, there are some things that should be done.

The best way to keep clients is to make certain that their needs are being met. This may sound obvious or simple, but in practice it is much more difficult. This is particularly true if you have a successful practice in which the needs of numerous clients bear down upon you at any given time. Nonetheless, being sensitive to client needs is the key to not only keeping clients, but also continuing to attract new clients via referrals from existing clients. A few more or less mechanical tools may be useful in ensuring that the obvious is not overlooked.

1. Ensure that you contact all of your clients periodically, regardless of whether you have any current work under-

way. If you have work underway, discuss that work with the client and make certain that their specific needs are reflected in your discussion. Unless the discussion is fairly specific, do not bill for this time. This contact is because you care about the client, not because you are attempting to generate billing time.

2. Attempt to communicate with active clients on a routine basis. This allows the client to know that you are concerned about them and that you are working on their behalf. These types of contacts also help ensure that there are no surprises. If you are not going to meet a promised deadline, let the client know as early as possible the reason for the delay and the new due date. If specific problems arise or if the result that the client wanted looks remote, use these discussions as a means to prepare the client for what is likely to occur. Clients do not like surprises. Use these contacts to ensure that they are not surprised.

3. Communicate with the client about billing matters. If bills are not being paid or paid on time, let the client know about your dissatisfaction and articulate clearly how you intend to proceed. If you feel that the bills are higher than expected, discuss the matter as early as possible with the client in order to avoid the surprise that will undoubtedly occur otherwise. If the client feels the bills are too high, offer to sit down immediately with him or her to discuss the matter.

4. Care about your clients. Life is too short to represent people or entities that you do not like, and in the end you will not be as effective in this type of representation. If you care about your clients, it will show in your work as well as in the success you will have in obtaining and maintaining clients.

    In this regard, I try to abide by a fairly simple creed. When problems with clients develop, "I never explain and I never complain." I just attempt to directly address the problem the best that I can. I do not attempt to explain because every explanation, no matter how legitimate I might believe it is, only sounds like an excuse to an upset client. I never complain. Clients simply do not care very much about your problems. Proceeding in this manner has allowed me to both keep clients I would have otherwise lost and, where necessary, to withdraw from representation with a minimum of problems.

I believe that another key to keeping clients is not to forget the proper role of a lawyer. As I have discussed earlier, in the practice of environmental law some view the issues involved from a moral perspective and, as a consequence, view certain positions as wrong and certain businesses as amoral. The environmental lawyer cannot afford to be in a position of engaging in this type of dialogue. In the end it will be counterproductive to the effective representation of client interests. The lawyer needs to concentrate on the job of being a lawyer. The key is to remember the role of the lawyer and to distinguish between your personal views and what is in the client's best interest. The idea is to be the lawyer, not the client. Proceeding with this in mind not only will enhance your client relations, but also make you much happier in the practice of law.

Expert Knowledge and Assistance

7

As NOTED EARLIER, THIS AREA OF THE LAW involves technical and complex issues that require a working knowledge of associated technical environmental fields. A lawyer practicing environmental law must be able to understand the nuances of various disciplines, including engineering, biology, toxicology, and chemistry. This knowledge must be fairly extensive and allow the lawyer to have intelligent and informed discussions with professionals and regulators with advanced degrees and working knowledge in these areas. There simply is no short-cut. The lawyer who does not understand the underlying factual predicate for the legal issues is simply not going to be able to adequately represent the client.

There are numerous ways you can gain the requisite knowledge. Some lawyers acquire it through the practical experience gained within governmental or corporate entities that regulate or that are part of the regulated communities. These lawyers not only learn the nature of the legal practice, but also learn the technical aspects through close proximity to those that have this type of substantive expertise.

A much more difficult means of obtaining the necessary levels of technical knowledge is through self-study and involvement with very basic issues. There are any number of technical courses offered for the lawyer who wishes to gain knowledge in specialized technical areas related to the practice of environmental law. These courses are usually taught by lawyers and technical experts who attempt to integrate the technical with the legal in a manner that facilitates learning by explaining why the technical is important to the practice of environmental law. Many of the courses are offered by tape and all have written materials that can be utilized to further strengthen skills.

Another way to learn underlying technical knowledge is to develop a working and ongoing relationship with various technical experts. You will need to develop this type of working relationship in any event, in order to prepare relevant comments associated with rulemakings and other administrative decision making, and to present evidence during administrative hearings or judicial litigation. I suggest that the relationship be developed well in advance of the need for client-specific information and work. Then you will not only have someone available to ask questions of and to learn from, but you will also have experts upon whom you can rely, ready to assist you when you need to use their skills. Moreover, you will have developed an on-going working relationship that should allow you to be much more efficient and effective in undertaking the client-related work that would be needed.

The first step, of course, is to develop an understanding of the disciplines that you will come in contact with in the area of environmental law in which you wish to specialize. This can be done over time through experience or through asking others who practice in the area in which you wish to specialize. In a similar way, you can meet individuals and firms within these technical disciplines through conferences, experience, or word of mouth.

Establishing an ongoing working relationship with experts in related environmental fields can also become the source of client referrals. Experts in related fields are quite often the first to come into contact with potential clients and often are in a position to refer those potential clients to a lawyer. The reverse is also true, with experts hired by lawyers to undertake critical investigations and to develop comments or testimony in aid of the client's interests.

I am aware that some engineers, biologists, toxicologists, and other technical, environmental experts became lawyers thinking that this will provide them with a substantial advantage over lawyers without technical training. In some respects this may be true. However, these technical lawyers run the risk of forgetting that they are lawyers. You cannot act in the capacity of a lawyer and a technical expert at the same time. The lawyer who also has an extensive technical background must decide to either be a lawyer or a technician. If you are going to be a lawyer, then you must look to another for technical advice.

There are countless examples of this type of problem. I remember, for example, litigating a case in which a government grant under the Clean Water Act was challenged based upon an alleged failure on the part of the grantee to develop and implement "alternative treatment technologies" to the sewer systems that had been selected. The plaintiff's lawyer presented motions and papers focused on the "new" technologies that might be available as an alternative to the sewer systems that were selected. At the time of trial, however, he offered no expert testimony to support his position, but rather attempted to make his point through argument.

The litigation concluded with a directed verdict at the end of the plaintiff's case. Later I learned that the lawyer, prior to being admitted to practice law, had been an engineer who fancied himself an expert in alternative treatment technologies with certain pet theories that he had advanced. In essence, he never became a lawyer—at least with respect to the subject litigation—but remained an "expert" to the ultimate detriment of his client.

In the more typical case where I have observed this problem, the lawyer's expertise acts to blind him or her to the weakness in the case or in the expert's testimony or qualifications. In preparation, the lawyer tends to mentally fill gaps with personal knowledge and fails to recognize that the lay jury or judge cannot do so; and the lawyer also often fails to see or hear problems with expert testimony because he or she is only half-listening to what the expert is saying, instead relying on personal expertise to fill gaps.

Long-Term Relationships 8

MATTERS IN THIS AREA OF THE LAW tend to take years to resolve. As a consequence, you need to be able to continue effective representation through the completion of the work involved. This requires some focus on at least two relationship issues.

First, you need to be able to deal with the bureaucracy and the regulators in such a manner that over time a working relationship is maintained. This is not easy. Regulators often view you and/or your clients in a less than favorable light. This view undoubtedly results from a combination of seeing a lot of real "bad actors" over time who make the same or similar representations with respect to their good faith efforts to do the right thing as the representations that you are making. This is often coupled with a bias that favors environmental protection at any cost. This latter bias stems from the reality associated with why you normally work within a regulatory agency in the first place, and perhaps a lack of any practical or true understanding or even interest in how the regulated community works. In any event, it is hard over the long haul to remain civil and work through and past all of the obstacles that are placed in the way of ultimate success for your clients. Nonetheless, if your practice involves working with regulators, you simply must be able to hang in there for the long haul.

Second, you need to be fairly comfortable that you like and trust your clients well enough to have a lasting and long-term relationship. This may seem like an obvious observation, but nothing can be worse than to be stuck in the middle of a protracted dispute with the regulators that you will need to deal with on behalf of other clients during the rest of your professional life, or to be in the middle of extensive and complex environmental litigation and discover that your client is someone whom you do not care for and whom you could care less about. At a minimum, it will affect how you represent the client's interests and, perhaps more importantly, how effectively you will be able to practice in the future. Think about this before, rather than after, you agree to proceed with representation.

A matter related to this second point revolves more or less around the specialized nature of the environmental law practice. As I have noted earlier, except in situations where the environmental law practice is a part of a larger more general practice, the work undertaken is limited; it does not include all of a client's legal needs. As a consequence, you must often work with other lawyers with a more general relationship with the client or with the client's corporate or general counsel. (Indeed, a great number of client referrals come from lawyers who serve this more generalized legal role.)

In this regard, I operate by a clear rule that first attempts to identify my role related to the other lawyer or lawyers involved. Once this is done, I determine if I am comfortable with the relationship. If I am not, I attempt to identify the problem and then discuss it with the other lawyer(s), and if necessary with the clients. In most cases, this discussion leads to adjustments in the relationship that is satisfactory to all concerned. In those rare cases where this has not occurred, I have declined to undertake representation or have withdrawn from further representation.

Once an understanding defining appropriate roles has been arrived at, along with appropriate lines of communication among myself, other lawyers involved, and the client, I operate consistent with that understanding.

My goal is not to put myself at odds with other lawyers also representing the client. Simply put, establishing bad relationships with other lawyers involved with representing mutual clients is bad for business since it alienates those lawyers and it then becomes unlikely that they will be a future source for work. It is also counterproductive to providing the most effective representation to the involved client.

In some respects, the foregoing is obvious. In practice, it can be one of the most frustrating experiences that you can have. I remember being retained by a large public body to represent it in some fairly complex litigation. The public body had very competent in-house legal counsel. This lawyer, however, was not a litigation lawyer and, in addition, identified so closely with the client that he had lost all perspective over the matter. He accepted the fact that I had been retained to lead the litigation effort, but nonetheless refused to refrain from attempting to micromanage the litigation.

I spent a great part of the first year of that litigation attempting to deal with this relationship problem. In that time, I had countless meetings with elected officials, management, and other affected parties in an attempt to deal with the problem. In that process, I wrote two of the oddest letters in my career. In the first, I used World War II analogies in an attempt to sort out relationships and appropriate roles, and in the other, I tried to explain the difference between "strategies" and "tactics" as a further means of defining appropriate relationships. In the end, the client finally asserted itself and instructed the in-house counsel in his proper role. The end result was the transformation of one of my worst litigation experiences to one of my best.

Litigating Environmental Law Cases 9

WHILE LITIGATION IS NOT UNIQUE to the environmental law practice, there are certain elements that require additional or perhaps more focused attention. Litigation tends to be technical in nature and trials can and often do last for several weeks or months. Considering this fact and accounting for it in the management of the environmental law practice are essential to the continued health and vitality of the practice.

Obviously, to the extent that you or other lawyers within the firm will be occupied for great periods of time in trial, it is important to have continued support—both lawyers and support staff—for other clients. My experience is that clients are more or less sympathetic to your need to focus on trial-related matters as you prepare for and litigate a case. The key is to communicate with clients, keep them informed of your progress, and make certain that there are others within the firm who are capable of handling specific matters that may arise when you are gone. Again, adequate advance preparation is the key.

Preparation for a long trial, of course, requires a certain amount of forethought to ensure that you have everything that you need and that support mechanisms are in place sufficient to allow you to focus on the actual litigation of the case. This is even more crucial if the trial is in a location removed from where you have an office.

Considerations for a Trial Close to Home

♦ Make certain clients have been contacted and that they are aware of the fact that you will not be available for an estimated period of time during normal working hours. Let them know whom they may contact if the need arises. Also, if necessary, make arrangements to speak with them or meet with them after normal business hours or on weekends.

♦ Arrange a time after trial each day to meet with other lawyers and support staff to discuss questions or other issues that have arisen during the day and to provide some direction regarding what needs to be dealt with on the following day.

♦ Arrange a time each day to check your mail, e-mail, and voice-mail. If possible, have others first review these communications and provide you summaries of what is there and copies of the most important items. Provide a time for returning telephone calls, if necessary, on the following day. My personal preference is to concentrate fully on trial matters during the day. Returning phone calls to clients during recess or at lunch detracts from the attention I otherwise like to give to the trial. Arranging a preset time after trial or on weekends to return or make essential telephone calls helps avoid this distraction during trial.

♦ Plan on spending at least an hour alone in your office after trial each day. This should allow you the time to think through other client needs so that you can provide adequate direction to others on how to deal with whatever issues have arisen. Do not make the mistake of assuming that you can carry on a full and vibrant practice "on the side" while you are attempting to litigate. You must rely upon others and plan in advance.

Considerations for a Trial at a Location Away from Home

Most of what was articulated above should be adopted for a trial away from home. The major differences, of course, are that face-to-face meetings among other lawyers and support staff are replaced with telephone conferences. However, in most other respects, the considerations are the same. Mail can be forwarded to you by overnight service, with the most crucial mail sent for your review through facsimile transmission.

Two general approaches to litigation away from home present themselves. The first is litigation in which you are associated with local counsel. In this situation, most of the support you need from office capability to library materials should be arranged and provided by the local firm. Indeed, these capabilities should head the list of considerations that you need to keep in mind when selecting local counsel.

The second situation is where you have no local counsel and need to establish your own capabilities away from home. There are a number of ways that you can take care of these needs, from subletting space or capability from a local firm or business to establishing a satellite office for the term of the trial. In large part, how you do this may depend upon the length of time at issue. The longer the trial, the more self-sufficient you will need to be.

One way of doing this is to rent an apartment or apartments to house lawyers and support staff. Rental furniture is relatively inexpensive and allows you to furnish your apartment in an eclectic home-office style. Bookcases, desks, and conference-type tables mix well with beds, sofas, and rented kitchen utensils. The idea here is to think practically. In the truest sense, you should furnish with the idea of living in your office. This means also furnishing the apartment with computer capabilities, fax machines, answering machines, and copy machines. This is not the best way to live but, in some respects, it is the best way to litigate. Everything you need to concentrate on the trial is at your fingertips from the time you wake up in the morning until the time you fall asleep at night.

Other options include hotels, residential suites, corporate housing companies, and furnished apartments. You will need to determine at what point it becomes more expensive to stay in a hotel or residential suite than to rent a furnished apartment or use the services of a corporate housing company. Corporate housing companies are not available in all areas. For a long stay, it may be more cost-effective to rent a furnished apartment.

A hotel, a residential suite, a corporate housing company, or a furnished apartment will each require a different level of involvement on your part for set-up of your physical location. No matter where you stay, though, some or all of the following factors should be considered:

- ♦ **Utilities.** Phone service, gas, electricity, water, and so on. A hotel or residential suite will provide this as part of your room, and a corporate housing company will set up these necessities. If you are renting an apartment, make sure the phone company, gas company, electric company, and water company are all notified in advance of your arrival, and a bill-paying account established. No matter what your housing, make sure you have an up-to-date copy of the phone company's White and Yellow Pages.

- ♦ **Additional Furniture.** You may need additional furniture no matter where you stay. You will probably need bookshelves or file cabinets to accommodate boxes and binders of documents you will need to bring with you. Although not the prettiest sight in the world, I've found that bookshelves work best, as you can see what you need at a glance, as opposed to leafing through file cabinet drawers. You may also need more chairs or a larger table for meetings with experts. Locate a local furniture-rental company to arrange for rental, delivery, and pickup of any additional furniture. Be sure to take physical measurements of the space where the furniture will be located so the furniture will actually fit. If you are in a hotel, find out their policy for bringing extra furniture into the room.

- ♦ **Linens.** A hotel and residential suite will supply linens, and a corporate housing company will arrange for them. Make sure a furnished apartment includes linens.

♦ **Kitchen Equipment.** A residential suite will include it, and a corporate housing company will arrange for it. Make sure a furnished apartment includes it. Know what you are willing to live without. For example, do you need a microwave oven? Not all housing types consider these part of their basic kitchen equipment.

♦ **Maid Service.** A hotel or residential suite will, of course, usually provide this on a daily basis. A corporate housing company's maid service schedule may vary, but is usually provided as part of their service. If a furnished apartment is rented, separate arrangements with a local maid service must be arranged, and a level of service must be agreed upon. How often should the maid service come, and when? Do you want them to change the linens only? Or to scrub floors and wash dishes, too?

♦ **TV and/or VCR.** A TV set is usually considered standard furniture in all of the above types of housing, but a VCR may be optional. Will you need a VCR during your stay? If so, make sure one is available to you in the housing you choose.

♦ **Laundry and/or Dry Cleaning Services.** These are available at a hotel or residential suite, and often available in corporate housing. If a furnished apartment is rented, make sure there are at least washers and dryers close by.

♦ **Copy Machine.** No matter what you decide for housing arrangements, an "in-house" copy machine is preferred. A desktop copy machine will probably not be sufficient for the amount of copying you will do. I have discovered you almost always end up copying more than you anticipated. For a good quality machine with an automatic feeder and sorter bins, you may end up with a longer rental term than you will actually need, but it is worth the extra money. (Most companies have a minimum rental period, which may exceed your out-of-town stay.) Be sure to inquire into their service abilities and when repairs are available. If you are in a remote location with no all-night copy shops, nothing will make your life more miserable than having your copy machine break down at 11:30 P.M.

♦ **Elevators.** Unless you are in a ground-floor room, an elevator is almost always a must in housing. Some copy-machine-rental and furniture-rental companies will not deliver a copy machine or furniture if it must be hauled up a flight of stairs. Plus, lugging heavy litigation briefcases up and down stairs day after day is grueling.

♦ **Fax Machine.** Although many computers today include internal fax modems, having a separate, freestanding fax machine is very convenient. Many hotels and residential suites include them in their business suites. Corporate housing companies can arrange for them. If you are in a furnished apartment, a fax machine can be rented, usually on a monthly basis, for a reasonable price.

♦ **Computer Equipment.** No matter where you stay, make sure there is a phone outlet for your modem near a comfortable working location with adequate light. Test your modem connection before you really need it. Not all phone wiring is created equal. Make sure the table on which you place your computer, printer, and scanner is a sturdy one.

♦ **Audio/Visual Equipment.** Determine what you will need, and if you want to take it from your office or rent it a the trial location. Even if you take what you think you will need from your office, find out what is available for rental at your trial location in case you decide to rent something later down the line.

♦ **Restaurant Delivery Services.** Determine what restaurant delivery services are available in your out-of-town location.

♦ **Map of Area.** Obtain a map of the area, and locate the nearest stationery store, gas station, and grocery store. Also, note the best route to and from your housing and the trial location, as well as an alternate route, just in case you need it.

♦ **Cancellation Policies.** Before you arrange for any of the above, make sure you have a clear understanding of their cancellation policies. What sort of cancellation notice is required? How soon must it be given? What happens to your deposit (if any) if you cancel before or after a certain time?

◆ **Insurance on Equipment.** No matter what your housing, make sure you obtain insurance to cover all the equipment you will bring from your office.

◆ **Moving to and from the Location.** Although you will rent as much as possible at the trial location itself, there will still be a substantial amount of material that will require moving to and from your office and the trial location. Determine how much will be moved, and whether or not it will be more cost-effective to rent a van for the entire length of the trial (for moving to and from the trial location and for traveling to and from court), or hiring a moving company.

The logistics of all of this is, of course, difficult. However, good support staff are the key to success. Legal assistants with litigation knowledge can work with you in the preparation and implementation of this strategy and good secretarial assistance, both back at the office and at trial on the road, will be the keys to your success. This relates back to some of the general considerations associated with support staff that were dealt with earlier.

As part of your general scheduling of time, you need to accommodate general trial preparation, including preparation of witnesses, preparation of cross-examination questions and, if necessary, the preparation of trial-related pleadings. Again, advance preparation of how all of this is to fit into your day, along with all of the non-trial-related matters, is important. My usual practice is to turn to non-trial-related matters directly after trial and to focus on trial preparation at dinner and afterward. I then return to non-trial-related matters before bed, with time for trial-related matters undertaken when I awake and before I return to court.

Making certain that other lawyers and support staff are properly occupied is equally important. In general, I think of this type of management in shifts with secretaries provided work late at night and in the late afternoon, with down time in between. I also assume that legal assistants will be my liaison between myself and secretaries, moving from the courtroom to the home-office as necessary.

The key, as noted earlier, is to treat your support staff as the professionals they are. Define their tasks and make certain that they understand your expectations and appropriate time deadlines for performance.

Conflicts/Ethical Problems 10

THE QUESTION OF CONFLICTS is also not unique to the environmental law setting and can, for the most part, be dealt with similarly to how they are dealt with in other areas of practice. The best way to start is to make certain that you have developed an internal practice that allows you to identify conflicts or potential conflicts early. The following, at a minimum, should be identified:

1. The name of client, including all aliases and business-related names.
2. The names of all individuals or entities that are likely to be on the other side of the transaction or litigation.
3. The names of all other relevant interested parties.
4. A description of the nature of the work that is to be undertaken.
5. A description of the facts that are involved as well as the general legal issues that may be involved.

In a firm other than a solo practice, this information needs to be circulated to all lawyers with written responses provided to the interested lawyer. Clear conflicts or potential conflict will be identified in this manner. However, it is also important to identify conflicts that are not as clear. The following should also be considered.

1. **Issues.** Conflicts in which there is no client conflict but where advocating and otherwise advancing an argument in favor of the prospective client may have an adverse effect upon other clients' interests. This situation has the potential to occur fairly often in the environmental law context. It is simply difficult to jump from an environmentally protective position to a position in which you represent the regulated community. Clients, regardless of their "side" in the environmental equation, do not like it.

2. **Plaintiffs versus Defendants Cases.** Closely related to issues conflicts are situations where a class of your clients are normally defendants, say in cost-recovery cases, and you have been approached with respect to the representation of a potential plaintiff. In this situation, advocating a plaintiff's position may have an effect upon the broader class of defendants in other actions.

3. **Representing Clients in Litigation against Regulatory Agencies.** A natural outgrowth of working with regulatory agencies is the fact that at times you may need to litigate against them. This, of course, places you in a fairly confrontational position with respect to the very people that, on behalf of other clients, you are attempting to work with. While some clients have no problem with this dual role of their lawyer, others become very uncomfortable.

In all of these situations and in others, the key is to be open with existing and prospective clients, explaining the potential litigation and its broader ramifications. I have on occasion raised concerns with prospective clients and asked if I can discuss my concerns with existing clients. Assuming that no objections have been raised, I have then had those discussions. I have had a variety of responses in these types of conversations and points that I had never considered on my own have caused me to rethink my original inclinations. I have even had the experience of having clients encourage me to undertake representation in spite of the potential ramifications. I have, however, never allowed a client to replace my role as the one to determine how to proceed in a given situation.

Location of Your Practice 11

THE PRACTICE OF ENVIRONMENTAL LAW can be undertaken to only cover issues at the local level or the state level or the federal level, or it can involve much broader coverage, including the representation of clients at all levels in various forums. How you want to position your practice in this regard is critical because it implicates varied considerations. In order to understand the importance of this issue you need to be concerned about what it is that you want to practice. For example, a regulatory practice requires you to be close to the regulator. However, there is regulation at all levels of government. As a consequence, you need to consider at what level or levels you want to practice and act accordingly. A practice that focuses on local land-use issues will, of course, involve different logistical questions than one that focuses on regional or state permitting issues. A practice that deals with numerous federal permitting issues results in still different concerns.

In a similar manner, you must also look at questions associated with the nature of your client base. A client base that is located in just one area presents a different situation than one that involves clients spread throughout a state, region, or the nation. Moreover, it is common today to represent clients with extra-national environmental problems that require an expanded concept of how those needs are best accommodated.

In any event, some attention needs to be given to logistical questions including the location of your practice and how client needs are going to be accommodated.

Local Practice

A local practice is one that is focused upon general environmental compliance. This type of practice might include the overseeing of environmental audits of property that is being sold or developed, or it may include the environmental review of numerous transactional documents. Assuming that problems are uncovered, this type of practice might also include the oversight of environmental compliance. This compliance work might include direction of other technical experts and negotiating compliance or other orders with the relevant regulators. In the case of significant problems, this type of practice could involve civil litigation associated with cost recovery and even criminal work associated with local or state prosecution. Local practice might also mean working with local regulators at the city or county department of health or even involve representation of clients in criminal matters brought by the local district attorney. These types of practices can be lucrative, but depending upon the size of the local area, they may be limited in scope.

Regional Practice

Most federal and state regulation is undertaken at a regional level. As a consequence, having a practice located within a close distance of regional offices allows you to be able to establish the type of regular contact and easy access that will allow you to offer something a bit extra and make you more attractive to clients who may want to retain a lawyer who can provide representation at this regional level. Moreover, having a firm located near these regional centers reduces the time and consequent costs associated with the need to travel to these locations. This is particularly true in those situations in which representation includes the need to attend and represent clients during multiple days of hearings. Having a regional practice, of course, also expands your potential client base.

State Level Practice

Just as many regulatory agencies are regionalized, many also have their main or a central office within the respective state capitols or, in the alternative, at or near major metropolitan areas. Location of a practice near these areas also provides for more or less regular contact and easy access to regulators that may be important to your clients' interests. In addition, similar to regional practices, because of the routine nature of the contact that is involved, location near these statewide offices reduces client and lawyer costs associated with travel. This is particularly true in the case of participation in extensive hearings or other on-going procedures. Again, a statewide practice allows you to further expand your client base.

Federal Level Practice

Finally, the focus of a lot of environmental law is Washington, D.C. As a consequence, many environmental law firms are located or have offices in Washington, D.C. This type of practice is very broad-based and, for the most part, seeks to influence decisions that may have industrywide impacts.

It May Not Matter

While location is and should be a factor in the nature of the type of environmental practice you undertake, in the long term it may not matter. In the age of facsimile, e-mail, telephone, and videoconferencing, and with the ability to travel quickly to different locations, you can probably establish a successful, broad-based, environmental practice from almost any location. Again, time and consequent costs are the most critical limiting factors in this regard. It is possible to deal with these matters through billing or other arrangements that serve as an equalizer to limitations that otherwise might create location limitations.

Related to this question is exactly where you are in your practice. For example, an established law firm with a practice that is being expanded into the area of environmental law may have the luxury of opening up small satellite offices at the regional, state, or federal levels. Similarly, an experienced lawyer also can relocate to areas away from these regional or state centers, having established both the requisite relationships and reputation to sustain this type of practice from a more remote location.

In addition to the pure business question of locating a practice are the consequent professional and personal questions that are involved.

First, the broader the scope of your practice, the more concerned you need to be about ensuring that your practice does not violate licensing or admissions requirements. Assuming that you are not practicing in a multistate, regional, or national firm, then these issues are of critical concern. One way of addressing these questions is through affiliation with local lawyers and law firms through whom you can practice. The rules in this regard change from jurisdiction to jurisdiction and you must be informed and abide by the relevant proscriptions. It is important to note that most of this broader representation stems from the federal aspects of the law that almost always requires clients to rely on a broader type of legal representation than otherwise might be expected.

These jurisdictional concerns also apply to the representation of clients in litigation. In the litigation context, most courts have specific rules with respect to admissions that will allow lawyers from other jurisdictions to practice, in at least a limited fashion, assuming certain minimal requirements are met.

Assuming that you have tackled all of the licensing and admissions questions and have dealt with the physical logistical and location problems associated with a broad environmental practice, you need to grapple with the personal issues. A broad practice involving local, regional, state. and federal representation is a practice that requires you to be away from home a great deal. As noted elsewhere, the practice of environmental law is time-intensive and issues and matters do not resolve quickly. As a consequence, you need to recognize the long-term and continual displacement this can cause.

My own practice developed quickly into one that included the representation of clients at the broadest levels. I never really thought about what would be required to maintain this type of a practice until the practice had been developed. As a consequence, I have spent hours and hours in traveling across the country and have literally spent years litigating environmental matters in areas remote from my home. I place no judgment on whether this is good or bad. I only note it here because some advance thought about whether this is the type of practice that you desire is probably better than to simply fall into the situation without any preparation.

A Last Word 12

I HAVE ATTEMPTED TO BREAK DOWN and analyze all of the steps that I and others with successful environmental law practices have taken, over the years, to start, build, and maintain those practices. I am fairly comfortable that I have done that, and that while there may be numerous variations that can and should be employed, the core of what is necessary to succeed has been covered in this book. In spite of this, I am uncomfortable that something much less tangible has been left out and should at least be considered and mentioned.

As I noted at the outset, key factors to success include being a skilled lawyer, a skilled environmental lawyer, and enjoying the practice of law. It appears to me that no matter how good you become at the mechanical steps outlined in this book, unless you are skilled as an environmental lawyer and enjoy the practice of law, your success, if it comes at all, will be limited.

Additionally, there is a need to understand that even being a skilled environmental lawyer who enjoys the practice of law may not be enough. The reality is that life is often not fair and all of the hard work you undertake just does not translate into the type of business success that is expected. In large part this has to do with the luck or circumstances surrounding your efforts. Being able to recognize that opportunities for success do not present themselves every day and, as a consequence, when they do present themselves they must be seized may be critical to the development of an environmental law practice, as is anything else that I have noted in this book.

I have been very fortunate in my own practice that, either as a direct result of my own efforts or otherwise, opportunities for client and practice development have presented themselves. However, once these opportunities have been presented, I have acted quickly and decisively to convert those opportunities into real clients and real business.

All of this is a long way of saying that luck does have a lot to do with success. Nonetheless, I am convinced that ultimately, regardless of how lucky you are, success can only be found in the hard work and rigor that I have discussed above. This is also where you can find the real satisfaction in the practice of environmental law.

Appendix A

SUMMARIES OF MAJOR ENVIRONMENTAL STATUTES

Dates first given are dates of first significant enactment. Later significant amendments may be noted. Statutory section references may use the familiarly-used original act numbers, as noted in West Publishing Company's annual Selected Environmental Law Statutes. State statutes are alphabetized by state; citations to treaties and conventions are listed in a separate section below.

Index to State and Federal Statutes

- APA, Administrative Procedures Act, 5 U.S.C.A. §501 et seq.
- CAA, Clean Air Act
- California—Proposition 65
- CERCLA, (Superfund), Comprehensive Environmental Response, Compensation, and Liability Act
- CWA, Clean Water Act
- CZMA, Coastal Zone Management Act of 1972
- EPCRA, Emergency Planning and Community Right to Know Act
- ESA, Endangered Species Act
- FEPCA, Federal Environmental Pesticide Control Act of 1972, *see* FIFRA
- FFDCA, Federal Food, Drug, and Cosmetics Act
- FIFRA, Federal Insecticide, Fungicide, Rodenticide Act
- Florida—Critical Areas Act
- FLPMA, Federal Land Policy and Management Act
- FOIA, Freedom of Information Act
- FQPA, Food Quality Protection Act of 1996
- FWPCA, Federal Water Pollution Control Act; *see* CWA
- Hazardous Substance Act, 15 U.S.C.A. §1261; *see* RCRA
- HAZMATTranport, Hazardous Materials Transportation Act
- Michigan—MEPA, Michigan Environmental Protection Act
- MMPA, Marine Mammal Protection Act
- Mining Act of 1872
- Mineral Leasing Act of 1920
- NEPA, National Environmental Policy Act
- NFMA, National Forest Management Act

- New Jersey—ECRA, Environmental Cleanup Responsibility Act
- New York—Forever Wild provision
- OPA '90, Oil Pollution Act of 1990
- Oregon—LCDC Act
- OSHA, Occupational Health and Safety Administration
- RCRA, Resource Conservation and Recovery Act
- Refuse Act/Rivers and Harbors Appropriations Act of 1899
- RRA, Resource Recovery Act of 1970; *see* RCRA
- SDWA, Safe Drinking Water Act
- SMCRA, Surface Mining Control and Reclamation Act
- SWDA, Solid Waste Disposal Act of 1965; *see* RCRA
- ToSCA, Toxic Substance Control Act
- Vermont — Act 250
- Watershed Protection and Flood Prevention Act
- Wild and Scenic Rivers Act
- Wilderness Act of 1964

Index to Some International Treaties, Conventions, and Resolutions

- Agenda 21, and *see* Rio Declaration
- Basel Convention on the Control of Transboundary Movements of Hazardous Wastes and Their Disposal
- Convention on Biological Diversity
- Convention on International Trade in Endangered Species of Wild Fauna and Flora (CITES)
- Desertification Convention
- European Community Directive on the Assessment on the Effects of Certain Public and Private Projects on the Environment
- General Agreement on Tariffs and Trade (GATT)
- Kyoto Protocol on Global Warming
- (International) — Montreal Protocol (on Stratospheric Ozone, pursuant to Vienna Convention for the Protection of the Ozone Layer)
- OECD Polluter-Pays Principle
- Resolution on Large-Scale Pelagic Driftnet Fishing and Its Impact on the Living Marine Resources of the World's Oceans and Seas

- Rio Declaration on Environment and Development
- Stockholm Declaration of 1972
- Straddling Fish Stocks Convention
- Treaty on the Non-Proliferation of Nuclear Weapons
- UNCLOS, United Nations Convention on the Law of the Sea

State and Federal Statutory Capsules

APA

Administrative Procedures Act, 5 U.S.C.A. §501 et seq. (1946). Passed virtually unanimously in 1946, the APA is the basic format statute for federal agencies' procedures for making law that affects persons outside the agencies (Title 5), and judicial review thereof (Title 7). It is binding on all federal agencies, and used as a model by most state administrative procedure codes and state courts' review thereof. Title 5 sets out some of the minimum procedural structures for rulemaking and adjudication (both can be done formally, with full TTP, trial-type-process, or informally), and the implicit basis for citizen participation therein. Informal rulemaking under §553 can be requested by any individual under §553(e). Agencies promulgate rules informally by notice-and-comment, with a Fed.Register Notice of Proposed Rulemaking, receipt and processing of written comments, and subsequent publication of a Notice of Final Rulemaking. Further formalization of rulemaking processes occurs with the voluntary or mandatory addition of hearings and other TTP. Title 7 creates a "generous review provisions" that should be given "a hospitable reception" in the reviewing courts. A valuable authoritative contemporaneous legal interpretation of all provisions of the APA is the U.S. Department of Justice, Attorney General's Manual on the APA (1946, reissued 1979). Amendments in the 1960s and 1970s added the Freedom of Information Act (§552) and the [less effective] Government-in-the-Sunshine Open Meetings Act (§552a).

CAA

Clean Air Act, 42 U.S.C.A. §§7521 et seq. (1970). Originally passed as 1970 Amendments to a weak prior federal law, the Clean Air Act

(CAA) is the leading example of a modern federal regulatory statute governing an environmental medium. Extensively amended in 1977 and 1990, it comprises several coordinated programs that address the major sources of air pollution in the United States. More specifically, it has programs that separately address stationary sources (Title I) and mobile sources of air pollution (Title III); it also has a separate program that addresses the control of hazardous air pollutants (§112). As the first statute of its kind it was and remains the principal model of what is usually referred to as a "command and control" statute. Title II controls mobile source pollution by setting maximum allowable tailpipe emissions for each type of vehicle (autos, light duty trucks, etc.), on a pollutant-by-pollutant basis as a function of the number of miles driven. For stationary sources, the CAA sets standards for emitters on a source-by-source basis, reverse engineered from a planning process that begins with National Ambient Air Quality Standards (NAAQSs) (health-based primary standards, and welfare [property and environment]-based secondary standards) that must be attained for the most common air pollutants. CAA, as a cooperative federalism statute, offers states the leading regulatory role so long as they enact and enforce programs that meet the federally mandated quality standards, under State Implementation Plans (SIPs) that prescribe the allowable emissions from stationary sources that will insure NAAQS attainment. Special sub-programs govern SIPs in areas of "nonattainment" of NAAQS quality levels, and areas to be regulated to prevent significant deterioration (PSD). As of 1990 the CAA implements a large-scale emissions trading program for sulfur dioxide emissions as part of the effort to combat acid deposition from long-range transport of that pollutant. A second major trading program to combat the effects of NOx pollution is in its formative stages.

Prop. 65

California "Proposition 65," Safe Drinking Water and Toxic Enforcement Act of 1986, Cal. Health & Safety Code §§25249 ff. (1990). All private businesses with more than ten employees must provide warnings with regard to consumer product exposures, occupational exposures, and environmental exposures to over 650 listed carcinogenic, mutagenic, and teratogenic substances. Carcinogens that pose "no significant risk" of contracting cancer and reproductive toxicants below a maximum risk level are exempted from tbe warning requirements. Warnings are required to be "clear and reasonble." Although Proposition 65 warnings have, in general, been inconspicuous and uninformative, the statute has been successful in achieving significant product reformulation and pollution prevention because of industry concerns about tort liability and consumer reactions to warnings.

CERCLA (Superfund)

Comprehensive Environmental Response, Compensation, and Liability Act, 42 U.S.C.A. §9601 et seq. (1980). Major amendment and reauthorization in 1986 known as tbe Superfund Amendments and Reauthorization Act (SARA). CERCLA is administered by EPA. Under CERCLA, Congress established the authority to remediate contamination from past waste disposal practices that now endanger, or threaten to endanger, public health or the environment. CERCLA does so primarily (1) by imposing strict liability on those parties responsible for the release of hazardous substances (§107); (2) by creating a "Superfund" to finance actions to clean up such releases (§111); and (3) by imposing the cleanup costs upon the parties who generated and handled hazardous substances. (§§107, 113.) CERCLA also empowers EPA to bring administrative or judicial enforcement actions against responsible parties to force them to perform site remediation. (§106.) In addition to establishing liability rules, CERCLA creates an administrative system to identify sites in need of environmental cleanups, to set priorities among cleanup efforts, to ensure that actions are taken on a site-by-site basis, and to require that planned responses are properly executed. (§105, 121.) CERCLA provides for civil and criminal penalties (CERCLA §103(b), (c), and (d)(2)), natural resource damages (§107(a)(4)(c)), and citizen enforceability (§310).

CWA

Clean Water Act, 33 U.S.C.A. §1251 et seg. (1972). Originally passed as 1972 Amendments to a weak prior federal law (FWPCA: the Federal Water Pollution Control Act), significandy amended in 1977 and 1987. Authorizes EPA to establish national, uniform technology based effluent limitations for point sources of pollution (e.g., factories and sewage treatment plants) discharging to waters of the United States, broadly defined to include wetlands. On waterways where technology-based limitations do not meet water quality standards based on fishable-swimmable quality, more stringent water quality-based effluent limitations must be imposed. Effluent limitations are enforced through the National Pollutant Discharge Eliminations System permit program, which has been delegated to 39 states. CWA §404 establishes another major permit program governing discharge of dredged and fill material into wetlands and other waters. The CWA does not apply to agricultural nonpoint source pollution (runoff), which accounts for approximately half of the water pollution in the United States. CWA §309 includes a wide range of civil and criminal enforcement mechanisms; and §505 contains a frequently used citizen-suit provision.

CZMA

Costal Zone Management Act of 1972, 16 U.S.C.A. §1451 et seq. (1972). A federal land-use planning statute that authorizes federal matching grants for assisting coastal states, including Great Lakes states, in the development of management programs for the land and water resources of their coastal zones. Once NOAA has approved a state's coastal management program as complying with minimum federal standards, additional federal matching funds become available for administering the program. CZMA contains a "consistency clause" mandating that any federal activity within a state's coastal zone be consistent with that state's approved coastal management program. CZMA §1455b, added in 1990, requires a state with an approved coastal management program to submit a Coastal Nonpoint Pollution Control Program for developing and implementing management measures to control coastal nonpoint source pollution.

EPCRA

Emergency Planning and Community Right to Know Act, 42 U.S.C.A. §1100 et seq. (1986). Establishes the Toxic Release Inventory (TRI), which requires certain manufacturing facilities to file annual reports with EPA that identify their use and release of one or more of 650 listed toxic chemicals above yearly threshold amounts. Results of this reporting are available on the Internet (TOXNET). Provides for a network of state and local emergency planning committees to facilitate preparation and implementation of emergency response plans.

ESA

Endangered Species Act, 16 U.S.C.A. §1531 et seq. (1973). Legislated in furtherance of CITES, the Convention on International Trade in Endangered Species. ESA is administered by DoI's Fish & Wildlife Service and Commerce's National Marine Fisheries Service. Under ESA§4 the Services place endangered and threatened species on the federal endangered species list, and prepare recovery plans. Under ESA§7 all federal agencies are forbidden to "jeopardize the existence" or destroy "critical habitat" of listed species, and must enter "consultation" with the Services when a Service's Biological Assessment shows that conflicts exist. Agencies can try to get "incidental take" exemptions from the Secretaries. By 1978 amendment a Cabinet-level "God Committee" is given power to issue exemptions after stringent findings of necessity and lack of alternatives. ESA§9 prohibits the "taking" of species by anyone, interpreted to include habitat destruction, thus reaching onto private property interests. By 1982 amendment ESA§10 allows petitioners to get exemptions via "incidental take" permits from the Secretaries, after going through procedures, including HCPs (habitat conservation plans), that can attach strict controls to private project actions if the Secretary so desires. ESA§11 provides severe criminal and civil penalties, and citizen enforceability.

FFDCA

Federal Food, Drug, and Cosmetics Act, 21 U.S.C.A. §301 et seq. (1938). The FFDCA is administered by the Food and Drug Administration (FDA, in the Department of Health and Human Services). The FFDCA prohibits the introduction or delivery into interstate commerce of any food, drug, device, or cosmetic that is adulterated or misbranded. The FFDCA regulates the occurrence of pesticide residues on raw agricultural commodities. The Delaney

Clause §409 prohibits additives that cause cancer when ingested by humans or animals, and until the FQPA of 1996 this was interpreted to include slightly carcinogenic pesticide residues in processed food as well. FFDCA violators face civil and criminal penalties.

FIFRA

Federal Insecticide, Fungicide, Rodenticide Act, 7 U.S.C.A. §135 et seq. (1972). In 1972, Congress passed the Federal Environmental Pesticide Control Act, which amended the first version of FIFRA passed in 1947 by establishing the basic framework for pesticide regulation. FIFRA is administered by EPA. FIFRA requires any person distributing, selling, offering, or receiving any pesticide to register with EPA (§3). EPA will grant registration upon the determination that (i) the pesticide is effective as claimed, (ii) the labeling and other data supplied by the manufacturer meet federal standards, and (iii) the pesticide will not cause unreasonable risks to humans or the environment, taking into account the economic, social, and environmental costs and benefits of intended use. Registrations must also be followed by establishing official tolerance levels that set the maximum permissible exposure for each chemical. Once granted, registrations act as perpetual licenses to market, although they can be cancelled or suspended upon an appropriate showing that a pesticide poses a substantial risk of safety or imminent hazard to man or the environment (§6). Other major amendments to FIFRA were passed in 1975, 1978, 1980, 1988, and 1996, which, in substance, shifted the statutory emphasis from labeling and efficacy to health and the environment and provided EPA with greater flexibility in controlling dangerous chemicals. FIFRA provides civil and criminal penalties (§14) but has no citizen enforceability provision.

Florida "Critical Areas" Act

Florida Environmental Land and Water Management Act of 1972, Fla. Stat. Ch. 380.06 (1972). The state legislature may designate certain environmental resources as "areas of critical concern." After designation, local development plans and regulations must be consistent with development principles established by the State Planning Agency. If local plans or regulations are not consistent with these principles, the State Administration Commission can override local authority and promulgate binding land-use plans and regulations for the area. Four areas, including the Big Cypress Swamp and the Florida Keys, have been designated to date. "Developments of regional impact" must be reviewed by Regional Planning Agencies if the relevant municipal plans and regulations have not been declared to be consistent with statewide planning goals.

FLPMA

Federal Land Policy and Management Act, 43 U.S.C.A. §1701 et seq. (1976). The current organic act for the Bureau of Land Management (BLM) in the Department of the Interior. Applies a multiple use, sustained yield management standard—including scenic, historic, ecological, and environmental uses—to a land-use planning process for allocating private access to the public lands, especially for grazing. Declares that the public lands will remain in public ownership, except where the national interest requires disposal or exchange. FLPMA establishes uniform disposal and exchange procedures. Although declaring that "fair market value" will be charged for private use of public lands, FLPMA, in practice, continues the preferential system of grazing permits and low grazing fees included in the Taylor Grazing Act of 1936.

FWPCA

Federal Water Pollution Control Act; *see* **CWA.**

FOIA

Freedom of Information Act, 5 U.S.C.A. §552 (1966). Provides that each agency state and publish in the Federal Register descriptions of its organization; location where the public may obtain information, make requests, or obtain decisions; nature of all formal and informal procedures; rules of procedure; statements of general policy adopted by the agency; and each amendment, revision, or repeal of the foregoing. Each agency shall make available for public inspection and duplication final opinions and orders made in the adjudication of cases; statements of policy not published in the Federal Register; and adminstrative staff manuals and instructions to staff that affect a member of the public. Fees for the furnishment of documents are limited to reasonable standard charges. Upon any request for records, each agency has ten days after the receipt of any request to determine whether to comply. Each agency has twenty days to determine whether to grant judicial review. Time limits may be extended only under "unusual circumstances." A request for records cannot be extended to matters (1) kept secret in the interest of national defense or foreign policy; (2) related solely to the internal personnel rules and practices of an agency; (3) specifically exempted from disclosure by statute; (4) trade secrets and commercial or financial information obtained from a person; (5) inter-agency or intra-agency memorandums or letters not generally available to the public; (6) disclosure of files which would constitute an unwarranted invasion of personal privacy; (7) records or information compiled for law enforcement purposes to the extent that the production of those records would interfere with an investigation or proceedings of law; (8) contained in or related to examination, operating, or condition reports prepared by or for the use of an agency responsible for the regulation or supervision of financial institutions; or (9) geological and geophysical information and data concerning wells.

FQPA

Food Quality Protection Act of 1996, Pub. L. No. 104–170, 110 Stat. 1489 (1996). Administered by EPA. Significantly amended both FIFRA and the Federal Food, Drug, and Cosmetic Act (FFDCA). Under FQPA, Congress did not comprehensively repeal the Delaney Clause, but did remove pesticide residues from its ambit by amending the FFDCA's definition of "food additive" (the Delaney Clause applies only to food additives) to exclude pesticide residues on raw or processed foods. In particular, Congress determined that a pesticide residue on such food is only to be considered unsafe if EPA has set a tolerance level for the substance and the residue fails to satisfy that level. The EPA is now allowed to grant a tolerance and register a pesticide upon a finding of safety (FQPA §405). Liberalized appeal rights for citizens is part of the compromise struck in eliminating the food additive ban.

HMTA

Hazardous Materials Transportation Act, 49 U.S.C.A. §§5101 et seq. (1976). HMTA is administered by the Department of Transportation. HMTA covers the transportation of all types of hazardous materials, regardless of whether they are raw materials, chemical intermediates, finished products, or wastes. In particular, HMTA governs the safety aspects of transportation, and requires the specification of containers, warning signs, and the like, complementing RCRA. §3003(b) provides that RCRA transporter regulations are to be consistent with DOT regulations under HMTA when the transportation of hazardous waste is subject to both Acts.

Hazardous Substances Act; *see* RCRA

MMPA

Marine Mammal Protection Act of 1972, 13 U.S.C.A. § 1361 et seq. (1972). Devised in response to a Congressional finding that some marine mammals were in danger of depletion or extinction. These mammals were found important to the ecosystem and warranted protection for the health and stability of the marine ecosystem rather than for commercial exploitation. The Secretaries of Commerce and of the Interior bear the responsibilities of this Act for their respective groups of mammals. Title I declares a permanent moratorium on the "taking" and importation of marine mammals or their products. Exceptions to this moratorium include (1) the "taking" of marine mammals for subsistence or for the manufacture of native clothing or crafts by Alaskan natives; (2) the "taking" of marine mammals for scientific research; and (3) additional one-year exceptions for those who might otherwise suffer undue economic hardship. Before the imposition of regulations, public hearings and publications of information are required. This Act directs the Secretary of the Treasury to ban the importation of fish or products caught in a manner that causes death or injury in excess of federal standards. Regulations are issued with regard to the "taking" and importation of marine mammals. Violation of regulations and provisions of this Act results in either civil penalties, criminal penalties, or both, but the Act provides no citizen enforcement provision.

Commerce and Interior Secretaries are responsible for enforcement, with assistance from the Coast Guard and state officers.

MEPA

Michigan Environmental Protection Act, M.C.L.A. §§1701 et seq. (1970). MEPA represented the legislative embodiment of Professor Joseph Sax's efforts to open up the process of environmental regulation and law to citizen initiatives. In 1994, the law was recodified in a process that intended no substantive changes, but which removed some of MEPA's broad language of citizen enforcement. Along with broad citizen standing provisions, MEPA has two extraordinary substantive aspects: it invites the courts of Michigan to create a common law of environmental quality under the aegis of the statute (which has been done), and it grants courts the authority to ignore or revise administrative standards that the court finds inadequately protective of the public trust in the state's air, water, and natural resources. The limitation of relief to injunctive relief and not awarding attorney's fees to successful plaintiffs are the most probable explanations of why the statute has not been used in large numbers of cases.

Mining Act of 1872

General Mining Law of 1872, 30 U.S.C.A. §22 ff. (1872). Governs hardrock mining on federal land. Declared all non-withdrawn federal land open to hardrock mineral exploration and extraction, without requiring payment of a fee to the United States. Established the system of "discovery-location-patent": (1) staking a mining claim entitles the claimant to an exclusive property right against all but the United States; (2) once a valuable mineral is located in a barely profitable quantity, the property right can be excercised even against the United States; and (3) after several years of negligible work and payment of a modest fee, the claimant can be granted a federal patent that gives him or her outright ownership of the former claim. Until fairly recently, federal land management agencies claimed to possess no statutory authority to regulate the environmental abuses caused by hardrock mining. Thus, abandoned and polluting mines are frequently encountered in the West.

Mineral Leasing Act of 1920

30 U.S.C.A. §181 ff. (1920). One of several federal statutes— including the Federal Coal Leasing Amendments of 1975, 30 U.S.C.A. §1201 et seq.—that removed fuel minerals from the ambit of the General Mining Law, and established a leasing system administered by the BLM. This statute required competitive bidding for oil leases on federal lands, including the outer continental shelf, and reasonable royalty payments to the federal government. The BLM is authorized to include lease provisions protecting the environment against potential damage caused by extraction and road construction.

NEPA

National Environmental Policy Act of 1969, 42 U.S.C.A. §4321 et seq. (1970). NEPA §102(2)(c) requires all federal agencies proposing to undertake major actions that might significantly affect the human environment to prepare and circulate Environmental Impact Statements (EISs). Under CEQ's NEPA regulations, Draft EISs (DEISs) must be made available to the public and other federal agencies possessing expertise regarding the proposal. The proposing ("lead") agency may not make irretrievable commitments of resources during the comment period and for 90 days after the publication of the Final Environmental Impact Statement (FEIS). NEPA does not contain a citizen-suit provision, but the courts have recognized a lawsuit for violation of NEPA's "procedural" obligations, i.e, the responsibility of the lead agency to make full disclosure of the proposal's alternatives and environmental impacts, as well as the agency's balancing process between environmental protection and economic development. Once full disclosure has been made, an agency decision to implement a proposal cannot be overturned in court unless it is found to be arbitrary and capricious.

NFMA

National Forest Management Act, 16 U.S.C.A. §1600 et seq. (1976). Applies a multiple use, sustained yield standard to management of the National Forests by the Forest Service (in the

Department of Agriculture). Establishes a planning program requiring the development of Land and Resource Management Plans (LRMPs), with which site-specific activities, such as timber sales, must be consistent. NFMA sets vague guidelines, replete with exceptions, for timber harvesting in general, and clearcutting in particular.

New Jersey ECRA

Environmental Cleanup Responsibility Act, N.J.S.A. 13: lK-6 ff. (1983). This statute administered by the New Jersey Department of Environmental Protection (DEP) ensures that when industrial properties are sold, any contamination will be discovered and remediated. ECRA applies only to industrial establishments with SIC Code numbers from 22 to 39 (industrial manufacturing), 46 to 49 (utilities), 51 (nondurable goods wholesaling), and 76 (miscellaneous repair services). ECRA is triggered by transactions such as sale, long-term lease, merger, bankruptcy, or closure. Prior to completing the transaction, the owner or operator must notify DEP, which determines the nature of site sampling that must take place before the transaction may be closed. The owner/operator must submit to DEP the sampling results, along with data regarding the history of the site, environmental permits and violations since 1960, hazardous materials stored onsite, etc. Depending on the condition of the site, the owner/operator must then submit a Negative Declaration or Cleanup (Closure) Plan to DEP for approval. If cleanup is necessary, DEP enters into an Administrative Consent Order with the owner/operator that sets cleanup schedules and ensures that financing (e.g., surety bonds) will be available for the cleanup. Owners and operators are strictly and jointly and severally liable for ECRA compliance. If ECRA is violated, DEP may void the transaction. However, ECRA has proven to be virtually self-executing in that financial institutions will not become involved in transactions that are not ECRA-compliant.

New York: Forever Wild provision

Forever Wild provision, McKinney's N.Y. Const. Art. 14, §1, (1894, amended 1995). This provision dictates that the lands of the state, now owned or later acquired, constituting the Adirondack Park forest preserve as now fixed by law, shall be forever kept as wild forest lands. These lands will not be leased, sold, or exchanged, or be taken by any corporation, public or private, nor shall the timber be sold, removed, or destroyed. A citizen may bring a suit alleging a violation of this provision pursuant to Article 14 §5.

OPA '90

Oil Pollution Act of 1990, 33 U.S.C.A. §§2701 et seq. (1990). First passed in 1990. Modeled on CERCLA, OPA is administered by EPA, in conjunction with the U.S. Coast Guard and the National Oceanic and Atmospheric Administration. Under OPA, Congress imposed strict liability upon owners or operators of vessels or facilities that discharge oil upon waters subject to United States jurisdiction, for cleanup costs and damages caused by such discharges (OPA §1002). However, Congress exempted cargo owners from such liability (OPA §1002). Facilities must develop spill prevention, control, and countermeasure (SPCC) plans, have them approved by EPA or the Coast Guard, and implement them, or face heavy civil and criminal penalties. OPA '90 explicitly does not preempt state oil spill cleanup laws. Congress also placed limitations on the extent of liability. Under OPA §1004, Congress increased the federal liability limit eight-fold (to $1,200 per gross ton) over the cap previously provided in §311 of the Clean Water Act. Congress also created a $1 billion Oil Spill Liability Trust Fund to pay for cleanup costs in excess of the liability limit, with up to $500 million available for payments for damages to natural resources (OPA §1012). Congress further disavowed any intent to preempt state liability requirements with respect to oil spill and removal activities (OPA §1018). OPA provides for civil and criminal penalties (OPA §§4301–4303) for natural resource damages (OPA §1006).

Oregon LCDC Act

Oregon State Land Use Act of 1973, Or Rev. Stat. §197 (1973). Established a seven-member Land Conservation and Development Commission (LCDC). All municipalities and counties must prepare comprehensive land-use plans, and adopt and enforce zoning ordinances that are consistent with the statewide planning principles set by the LCDC. Nonconforming local plans or regulations may be rejected by the LCDC.

OSHA

Occupational Health and Safety Administration, 29 U.S.C.A. §651 et seq. (1970). Under OSHA, employers are required to furnish a workplace free from recognized hazards that cause or are likely to cause death or serious physical harm to employees (§5). This act charged the Secretary of Labor with the responsibility of promulgating national consensus safety standards and established federal safety standards (§6). An employer may apply to the Secretary of Labor for a "temporary order" granting a variance from a standard or any provision under this section, establishing that (1) he is unable to comply with a standard because of an unavailability of professional or technical personnel, materials, and equipment needed to come into compliance with the standard, or because necessary construction or alteration of facilities cannot be completed by the effective date; (2) he is taking all available steps to safeguard his employees against the hazards covered by the standard; and (3) he has an effective program for coming into compliance with the standard as quickly as practicable. The Secretary of Labor can establish emergency standards when employees are exposed to grave dangers from toxic materials or new hazards. Under §8, federal inspections and investigations of working conditions are authorized. Employees can request an inspection if they believe a safety or health violation exists in the workplace. If an employer is in violation of a standard, a federal inspector is authodzed to issue a citation (§9). Section 17 outlines civil penalties for serious violations and willful or repeated violations. The Secretary of Labor can approve a state plan to develop and enforce standards if the plan is found in compliance with OSHA (§18).

RCRA

Resource Conservation and Recovery Act of 1976, 42 U.S.C.A. §6901–6992(k) (1976). RCRA is administered by EPA. RCRA Subtitle C directs EPA to establish regulations ensuring the safe management of hazardous waste from "cradle to grave," in order to eliminate endangerment from present and future waste disposal

(§3001)("non-hazardous" waste is much less regulated, under Subtitle D). RCRA was reauthorized and substantially amended by the Hazardous and Solid Waste Amendments of 1984 (HWSA), which imposed new technology-based standards on landfills handling hazardous wastes, required the phaseout of land disposal for certain untreated wastes, and increased federal authority over disposal of nonhazardous solid wastes. In creating "cradle to grave" regulation over hazardous waste, RCRA attempts to regulate all aspects of the lifecycle of hazardous waste. RCRA does so by creating a tracking system that follows hazardous waste from the time of generation through treatment, storage, and disposal (§3002–4). RCRA also authorizes EPA to engage in corrective action that can prevent or remedy the release of hazardous wastes (§7003). EPA is authodzed to seek significant civil and criminal penalties (§3008). RCRA also provides for citizen enforceability (§7002).

Refuse Act

Refuse Act/Rivers and Harbors Appropriations Act of 1899, Pub. L. 97-322, 33 U.S.C.A. §40 ff. (1899). A statute passed at the end of the nineteenth century to facilitate the Corps of Engineers' mission to keep navigation channels free of obstruction. Section 407 forbade deposit without a permit of refuse in (or on the banks of so as to be washed into) any navigable river or any tributary thereto, which covers virtually the entire United States. Other sections required permits for physical alterations to watercourses. Section 411 sets criminal penalties, and a reward for informants who report violations. When in the twentieth century the word "refuse" came to be commonly defined to include pollution, the act became the first effective public law weapon against pollution. Its enforcement federalized the field and changed the way industry regarded pollution. To moderate some of the harshness of the Refuse Act, Congress passed the Clean Water Act of 1972 with far tougher standards than otherwise would have been likely, replacing some but not all of the Refuse Act's authority in the field. Federal prosecutors use the act in cases of grave intentional discharges into water bodies.

SDWA

Safe Drinking Water Act, 42 U.S.C.A. §3007 et seq. (1974). The SDWA regulates purveyors of potable water. It authorizes EPA to promulgate technology-based primary and secondary drinking water regulations, containing maximum contaminant levels (MCLs), applicable to public water systems, defined as systems that provide water to at least 25 individuals. Primary enforcement responsibility under the SDWA is delegated to states. The SDWA bans new installations of lead drinking-water pipes, protects "sole source aquifers" from inconsistent federal actions, and contains a major regulatory program applicable to underground injection of hazardous wastes. With regard to funding, the SDWA authorizes federal grants to states for (1) improving state drinking water regulation, (2) establishing revolving loan funding mechanisms for low-interest loans to upgrade public water systems, and (3) facilitating state planning for the protection of wellhead areas.

SMCRA

Surface Mining Control and Reclamation Act, 30 U.S.C.A. §1201 et seq. (1977). SMCRA established the Office of Surface Mining Reclamation and Enforcement in the Department of Interior, charged with administering the act's regulatory and reclamation programs, and providing grants and technical assistance to the states. Title IV establishes a self-supporting Abandoned Mine Reclamation Fund to restore land adversely affected by past uncontrolled mining operations. Titles IV and V provide that the state and federal governments are jointly responsibile for acquiring lands and enforcing environmental protection regulations required by the act. Under Title V, performance standards are set for environmental protection to be met by all major surface mining operations for coal. Title VI protects certain lands regarded as unsuitable for suface mining.

SWDA

Solid Waste Disposal Act of 1965, 42 U.S.C.A. §6901 et seq.; *see* **RCRA.**

ToSCA

Toxic Substance Control Act, 15 U.S.C.A. §2601 et seq. (1976). ToSCA is administered by EPA, and places on manufacturers the responsibility to provide data on the health and environmental effects of chemical substances, and provides EPA with comprehensive authority to prohibit the manufacture, distribution, or use of chemical substances that pose unreasonable risks. ToSCA also requires premanufacture notification of EPA for new chemicals or sigmficant new uses of chemicals. To implement these goals, EPA has the authority (1) to require the testing of chemicals (ToSCA §4), (2) to require the premanufacture review of new chemical substances (ToSCA §5), (3) to limit or prohibit manufacture, use, distribution, and disposal of chemicals (ToSCA §6), and (4) to require recordkeeping and reporting (ToSCA §8). ToSCA provides for civil and criminal penalties (ToSCA §16) as well as citizen enforceability (ToSCA §20).

Vermont Act 250

Vermont State Land Use and Development Act of 1970, Vt. Stat. Ann. Tit. 10 §6001 et seq. (1970). All developers of public or private construction projects of more than ten acres, and residential units of more than ten units, must obtain a project permit from one of nine regional Environmental District Commissions (EDCs). A permit may be denied if it is "detrimental to the public health, safety, or general welfare." The burden is on the applicant to prove that the project will not cause undue environmental degradation. Project opponents bear the burden of proving unreasonable burden on infrastructure or damage to aesthetic or historic sites. A developer must obtain an EDC permit before applying for other necessary local development permits. See Richard Brooks's two-volume treatise, *Toward Community Sustainability: Vermont's Act 250* (1997).

Watershed Act

Watershed Protection and Flood Prevention Act, 16 U.S.C.A. §1001 et seq. (1954). The act initiates a program where the Secretary of Agriculture cooperates with states and local agencies in the construction and financing of comprehensive soil conservation, flood prevention, and water control projects for small watersheds (§3). Under Section 4, the Secretary of Agriculture is permitted to determine the "proportionate share" of federal assistance that local organizations would receive for such projects. Under Section 5, the President issues rules and regulations necessary to carry out the purposes of the act, and coordinates the projects under this act with existing programs.

WSRA

Wild and Scenic Rivers Act, 16 U.S.C.A. §1271 et seq. (1968). The WSRA establishes the Department of the Interior's Federal Wild and Scenic Rivers System, including approximately 10,000 miles of designated wild, scenic, and recreational rivers and their corridors within one-quarter mile of each river bank. Dams are prohibited on designated rivers and their tributaries, and all federal activities must be consistent with the river's wild and scenic character. Federal lands abutting designated rivers must also be managed in a consistent manner. The WSRA contains no authority for federal regulation of private activities within the corridor of a designated river, and federal condemnation powers within the corridor are severely limited.

Wilderness Act of 1964

16 U.S.C.A. §1131 et seq. (1964). Establishes the Wildemess System, including extensive Wildemess Areas where all commercial logging and permanent roads and most structures and installations, temporary roads, commercial enterprises, mining, grazing, and use of motorized equipment are prohibited. The following secondary uses are permitted: logging to control insect infestations and fires; mineral exploration; mining claims, mineral leases, and grazing permits obtained before January 1, 1964; commercial services provided by guides, packers, and river runners; and hunting and fishing. The Departments of Interior and Agriculture are the primary agencies. Each addition to the Wilderness System must be made by specific congressional enactment.

Some International Treaties, Conventions, and Resolutions—Citations

Agenda 21; *see* Report of the UNCED at Rio de Janeiro, June 3–14, 1992
United Nations Conference on Environment and Development, Agenda 21, U.N. Doc. A/CONF. 151/26 (1992); reprinted in The Earth Summit: The United Nations Conference on Environment and Development (UNCED) 125-508 (Stanley P. Johnson ed. 1993). See also for annotations, Agenda 21: Earth's Action Plan Annotated (Nicholas A. Robinson ed. 1993).

Basel Convention on the Control of Transboundary Movements of Hazardous Wastes and Their Disposal, March 22, 1989
United Nations Environment Programme, UNEP/IG.80/3, March 22, 1989; reprinted in 28 I.L.M. 657 (1989).

Convention on Biological Diversity; *see* Report of the UNCED at Rio de Janeiro, June 3–14, 1992
United Nations Convention on Biological Diversity, June 5, 1992, S. Treaty Doc. 20 (1993); reprinted in 31 I.L.M. 818 (1992).

Convention on International Trade in Endangered Species of Wild Fauna and Flora (CITES), March 3, 1973
27 U.S.T. 1087, 999 U.N.T.S. 243; reprinted in 12 I.L.M. 1085 (1973).

Desertification Convention
International Convention to Combat Desertification in Those Countries Experiencing Serious Drought and/or Desertification, Particularly in Africa, June, 17, 1994, U.N. General Assembly Doc. A/AC. 241/15/Rev. 7 (1994); reprinted in 33 I.L.M. 1328 (1994).

European Community Directive on the Assessment on the Effects of Certain Public and Private Projects on the Environment
Directive on the Assessment on the Effects of Certain Public and Private Projects on the Environment, Council Directive 85/337/EEC, 1985 O.J. (L 175/40); 28 Official Journal of E.C. 40 (1985) L-175.

General Agreement on Tariffs and Trade (GATT), October 30, 1947
T.I.A.S. No. 1700, 61-V Stat. All, 4 Bevans 639, 55 U.N.T.S. 18: Arts. I, III, IX, XI, XX.

Kyoto Protocol on Global Warming
Kyoto Protocol to the FCCC, FCCC Conference of the Parties, 3d Sess., UN Doc. FCCC/CP/1997/L.7/ Add.l (Dec. 10, 1997); reprinted in 37 I.L.M. 22 (1998). Final version was issued as part of the Third Conference of the Parties Report, UN Doc. FCCC/CP/1997/7/Add.2.

Montreal Protocol
Montreal Protocol on Substances That Deplete the Ozone Layer, Sept. 16, 1987, S. Treaty Doc. No. 100-10 (1987); reprinted in 26 I.L.M. 1550.

Pursuant to Vienna Convention for the Protection of the Ozone Layer
Vienna Convention for the Protection of the Ozone Layer, Mar. 22, 1985, U.N. Doc. UNEP/Ig.53/Rev.l, S.Treaty Doc. No. 99-9, 99th Cong., 1st Sess. (1985), T.I.A.S. 11097; reprinted in 26 I.L.M. 1529.

OECD Polluter-Pays OECD Doc. C(72) 128
OECD Council Recommendations on Guiding Principles Concerning International Economic Aspects of Environmental Policies, adopted May 26, 1972, OECD Doc. C(72)128, Annex A(a) in Organisation For Economic Co-operation and Development, OECD and the Environment 24 (1986). Also available at 1972 WL 24710 (Int'l Envtl L. Library).

Resolution on Large-Scale Pelagic Driftnet Fishing and Its Impact on the Living Marine Resources of the World's Oceans and Seas
G.A. Res. 46/215, U.N. GAOR, 46th Sess., U.N. Doc. A/RES/46/215 (1992), Dec. 20, 1991; reprinted in 31 I.L.M. 241 (1992).

Rio Declaration on Environment and Development, June 13,1992
UNCED Doc. A/CONF.151/5/Rev. 1, June 13, 1992; reprinted in 31 I.L.M. 874 (1992); and Agenda 21.

Stockholm Declaration of 1972
Stockholm Declaration of the United Nations Conference on the Human Environment, June 16, 1972, Principle 21, U.N. Doc. A/Conf. 48/14 (1972), 11 I.L.M. 1416 (1972).

Straddling Fish Stocks Convention
Agreement for the Implementation of the United Nations Convention of the Law of the Sea of 10 December 1988, Relating to the Conservation and Management of Straddling Fish Stocks and Highly Migratory Fish Stocks, U.N. GAOR, 6th Sess., pt. x, art. 34, U.N. Doc. A/CONF. 164/37 (1995), reprinted in 34 I.L.M. 1542 (1995).

Treaty on the Non-Proliferation of Nuclear Weapons, July 1, 1968
21 U.S.T. 483, 729 U.N.T.S. 161; reprinted in 7 I.L.M. 811 (1968): Art. III.

UNCLOS, United Nations Convention on the Law of the Sea, October 7,1982
United Nations, Official Text of the United Nations Convention on the Law of the Sea with Annexes and Index, U.N. Sales No. E83.v.5 (1983); see also U.N. Doc. A/Conf. 62/122; reprinted in 21 I.L.M. 1261 (1982).

Appendix B

GLOSSARY OF ACRONYMS AND ABBREVIATIONS

AAIA	Airport and Aviation Import Act
ABEL	Ability to pay for environmental liability, both pollution controls and civil penalties
ACE	Any Credible Evidence rule (CAA)
ACO	Administrative Consent Order
ACRS	Advisory Committee on Reactor Safeguards
ADR	Alternate Dispute Resolution
AEC	Atomic Energy Commission (now NRC)
AICPA	American Institute of Certified Public Accountants
AID	U.S. Agency for International Development
AMPs	Allotment management plans (grazing)
ANPR	Advanced Notice of Proposed Rulemaking
APA	Administrative Procedures Act
AQCR	Air Quality Control Regions (CAA)
AR	Attributable Risk
ARARs	Applicable, Relevant, Appropriate Requirements (CERCLA)
ASTM	American Society for Testing and Materials
BACT	Best Available Control Technology
BADT	Best Adequately Demonstrated Pollution Control Technology (CWA)
BANANA	Build Absolutely Nothing Anywhere Near Anybody (*see* NIMBY)
BAT	Best Available Technology, or Best Available Technology Economically Achievable (CWA)
BCT	Best Conventional Control Technology (CWA)
BDAT	Best Demonstrated Available Technology (RCRAI)
BECC	Border Environmental Cooperation Commission (NAFTA)

BEN	EPA computer modeled value to determine the economic benefit of noncompliance
BLM	Bureau of Land Management (DoI)
BMP	Best Management Practices
BNA	Bureau of National Affairs
BOD	Biological Oxygen Demand (CWA)
BPJ	Best Professional Judgment (CWA)
BPT	Best Practicable Control Technology Currently Available (CWA)
BRZ	Biological Resource Zones (BRZMA)
BRZMA	Biological Resources Zone Management Act
CAA	Clean Air Act
CAFO	Concentrated Animal Feeding Operation
CAL-LEVs	California-Low-Emission Vehicles
CAM	Compliance Assurance Monitoring (CAA)
CAMU	Corrective Action Management Unit (CERCLA)
CAP	Capacity Assurance Plan (RCRA)
CARB	California Air Resources Board
CBE	Citizens for a Better Environment
CBF	Chesapeake Bay Foundation
CBO	Congressional Budget Office
CCC	California Coastal Commission
CDC	Center for Disease Control
CEC	Commission on Environmental Cooperation (NAFTA)
CEM	Continuous Emission Monitors
CEQ	Council on Environmental Quality (Executive Office of the President)
CEQA	California Environmental Quality Act
CERCLA	Comprehensive Environmental Response, Compensation, and Liability Act (Superfund)
CERCLIS	CERCLA Information System
CERES	Coalition for Environmentally Responsible Economics

CFCs	Chlorofluorocarbons
CFR	Code of Federal Regulations
CGL	Comprehensive General Liability insurance
CITES	Convention on International Trade in Endangered Species
CMA	Calcium Magnesium Acetate (road salt substitute), or Cooperative Management Agreement (PRIA)
CMP	Coastal Management Plan (CZMA)
COD	Chemical Oxygen Demand
COE, or Corps	U.S. Army Corps of Engineers
COG	Council of Governments (regional planning)
Corps	U.S. Army Corps of Engineers
CSD	Commission on Sustainable Development
CSI	Common Sense Initiative (EPA compliance-assistance program)
CSO	Combined Sewer Overflows (CWA)
CWA	Clean Water Act (FWPCA)
CZMA	Coastal Zone Management Act
DEC	Department of Environmental Conservation (various states)
DEIS	Draft Environmental Impact Statement (NEPA)
DEQ	Department of Environmental Quality (various states)
DMRs	Discharge Monitoring Reports (CWA)
DNR	Department of Natural Resources
DoA	U.S. Department of Agriculture
DoI	U.S. Department of Interior
DoJ	U.S. Department of Justice
DoT	U.S. Department of Transportation
DWP	Department of Water and Power (state level)
EA	Environmental Assessment (NEPA)
EAJA	Equal Access to Justice Act
EBEs	Environmentally Beneficial Expenditures (CWA)

EC	European Community
ECJ	European Court of Justice
EDF	Environmental Defense Fund
EIS	Environmental Impact Statement (NEPA)
ELP	Environmental Leadership Program
ELR	Environmental Law Reporter (by Environmental Law Institute)
EO	Executive Order
EPA	U.S. Environmental Protection Agency
EPCRA	Emergency Planning and Community Right-to-Know Act
EPCRTKA	EPCRA
ERC	Emission Reduction Credits (CAA), or BNA Environmental Reporter—Cases
ERDA	Energy Research and Development Commission
ESA	Endangered Species Act
ESD	Explanation of significant differences (CERCLA)
FACA	Federal Advisory Committee Act
FACE	For a Cleaner Environment (Woburn citizen group)
FASB	Financial Accounting Standards Board
FDA	U.S. Food and Drug Administration
FDF	Fundamentally Different Factors (CWA)
FEIS	Final Environmental Impact Statement (NEPA)
FELA	Federal Employers' Liability Act
FEPCA	Federal Environmental Pesticide Control Act
FERC	Federal Energy Regulatory Commission
FFDCA	Federal Food, Drug, and Cosmetics Act
FHWA	Federal Highway Administration
FIFRA	Federal Insecticide, Fungicide, Rodenticide Act
FIP	Federal Implementation Plan (CAA), as in "the state's SIP got shot down, and the state got FIPped"
FLPMA	Federal Land Policy and Management Act

FOE	Friends of the Earth
FOIA	Freedom of Information Act
FONSI	Finding of No Significant Impact (NEPA)
Form R	A toxic chemical Release Inventory Reporting Form (EPCRA); TRI information must be filed on a "Form R"
FORPLAN	A computerized model to determine LRMPs
FPC	Federal Power Commission
FQPA	Food Quality Protection Act of 1966
FR	Federal Register
FRCP	Federal Rules of Civil Procedure
FS	U.S. Forest Service (DoA)
FSEIS, or FEISS	Final Supplemental EIS
FWPCA	Federal Water Pollution Control Act (CWA)
FWS	U.S. Fish and Wildlife Service (DoI)
GAAP	Generally Accepted Accounting Principles
GAO	General Accounting Office (Comptroller General, congressional)
GATT	General Agreement on Tariffs and Trade
GDP	Gross Domestic Product
GI-GO	Garbage In-Garbage Out, as in cooking the data in USFS planning documents
GNP	Gross National Product
HCFCs	Hydrochlorofluorocarbons
HCPs	Habitat Conservation Plans
HCs	Hydrocarbons
HEW	U.S. Department of Health, Education, and Welfare
HMTA	Hazardous Materials Transportation Act
HREC	Hampton Roads Energy Company
HRS	Hazard Ranking System (CERCLA)
HRSD	Hampton Roads Sanitary District, a regional sewerage facility in Virginia
HSWA	Hazardous and Solid Waste Amendments (of 1984)

HWIR	Hazardous Waste Identification Rule
I & M	Inspection and Maintenance (CAA auto and truck emissions)
ICJ	International Court of Justice (The Hague)
ICOLP	International Cooperative for Ozone Layer Protection
ICS	Individual Control Strategy (CWA)
IEL	International Environmental Law
IGO	Intergovernmental organization
IJC	International Joint Commission (US–Canada)
ILM	International Legal Materials document series
ILO	International Labor Organization
Industrial Chemical Survey	(ToSCA)
IPM	Integrated Pest Management
ISC	Interagency Scientific Committee (ESA)
ISO	International Standards Organization
ISTEA	Intermodal Surface Transportation Efficiency Act
ITC	Interagency Test Committee (ToSCA), or Interagency Testing Committee
IWC	International Whaling Commission
LAER	Lowest Achievable Emissions Rate (CAA)
LAs	Load Allocations (CWA)
LCA	Life Cycle Assessment
LCCA	Lead Contamination Control Act (SDWA)
LCDC	Land Conservation and Development Commission (Oregon)
LDCs	Less-Developed Countries
LDRs	Land Disposal Restrictions (CERCLA)
LEVs	Low-Emission Vehicles
LG&E	Louisville Gas & Electric
LI	Environmental Law Institute
LOS	Law of the Sea (treaties), also UNCLOS
LRMPs	Land and Resource Management Plans (NFMA)
LUBA	Land Use Board of Appeals

LULU	Locally Undesirable Land Use (*see* NIMBY)
LUST	Leaking Underground Storage Tank
MA	Materials Accounting
MACT	Maximum Available Control Technology
MBTA	Migratory Bird Treaty Act
MCL	Maximum Contaminant Level (CWA)
MCLG	Maximum Contaminant Level Goals (CWA)
MD&A	Management's Discussion and Analysis
MDA	Medical Device Amendments
MDB	Multilateral Development Bank
MEPA	Michigan Environmental Protection Act
MMT	Million Metric Tons
MoA	Memorandum of Agreement
MoU	Memorandum of Understanding
MPCA	Minnesota Pollution Control Agency
MPO	Metropolitan Planning Organization (ISTEA)
MSW	Municipal Solid Waste
MUSY	Multiple Use-Sustained Yield Act
NAAQS	National Ambient Air Quality Standards
NACEPT	National Advisory Council for Environmental Policy and Technology
NADBank	North American Development Bank (NAFTA)
NAFTA	North American Free Trade Agreement
NAM	National Association of Manufacturers
NASQUAN	National Ambient Stream Quality Accounting Network (CWA)
NCP	National Contingency Plan (Superfund)
NED	New England Development Company
NEPA	National Environmental Policy Act
NESHAP	National Emissions Standards for Hazardous Air Pollutants (CAA)
NFMA	National Forest Management Act
NGO	Non-Governmental Organization
NGPRP	Northern Great Plains Resources Program

NIFYE	Not In My Front Yard Either (*see* NIMBY)
NIMBY	Not In My Back Yard! Syndrome
NIMTOO	Not In My Term Of Office (*see* NIMBY)
NLEV	National Low-Emission Vehicles
NMFS	National Marine Fisheries Service
NOAA	National Oceanographic and Atmospheric Administration (Department of Commerce)
NOEL	No Observable Effect Level (California)
NOPE	Not On Planet Earth (*see* NIMBY)
NOV	Notice of Violation
NPDES	National Pollutant Discharge Elimination System (CWA)
NPL	National Priority List (Superfund)
NPS	National Park Service
NRC	U.S. Nuclear Regulatory Commission, or (state) Natural Resources Commission
NRDC	National Resources Defense Council
NSF	National Science Foundation
NSPS	New Source Performance Standards (Air)
NTAs	Negotiated Test Agreements (ToSCA), or Negotiated Testing Agreements
NWF	National Wildlife Foundation
NWP	Nationwide Permit (CWA)
NWQS	National Water Quality Standards (CWA)
O&M	Operation and Maintenance
OCR	EPA's Office of Civil Rights
OCS	Outer Continental Shelf
ODA	Official Development Aid
OECD	Organization for Economic Cooperation and Development
OMB	Office of Management and Budget (Executive Office of the President)
ONRW	Outstanding National Resource Waters
OOMBY	Out Of My Back Yard (*see* NIMBY)

OPA	Oil Pollution Act of 1990
ORV	Off-Road Vehicle
OSHA	Occupational Safety and Health Act, Occupational Safety and Health Administration
OSWER	Office of Solid Waste and Energy Response
OTA	Office of Technology Assessment (congressional)
OTAG	Ozone Transport Assessment Group
OTC	Ozone Transport Commission (mobile sources)
PCBs	Polychlorinated biphenyls
PCSD	President's Council on Sustainable Development
PIL	Public Interest Litigation
PLLRC	Public Land Law Review Commission
PMNs	Pre-Marketing Notifications (ToSCA), or Premarket Notifications (ToSCA)
PNSCP	Pre-Notice Site Cleanup Program (CERCLA), or Pre-Notice Site Cleanup Program (Illinois EPA)
POCLAD	Program on Corporations, Law, and Democracy
POTW	Publicly Owned Treatment Works (CWA)
PPA	Pollution Prevention Act
PRIA	Public Rangelands Improvement Act
PRP	Potentially Responsible Party (Superfund)
PSD	Prevention of Significant Deterioration
QNCR	EPA's Quarterly Noncompliance Reports, e.g., on water pollution permit violations
RAC	Resource Advisory Council
RACHEL	Reauthorization Act Confirms How Everyone's Liable (SARA's unofficial alternate name)
RACM	Reasonably Available Control Measurements (CAA)
RACT	Reasonably Available Control Technology (CAA)
RAM	Real-time Air-quality-simulator Model
RAP	Refuse Act Program permit
RARE I, II, III	Roadless Areas Review and Evaluation (Wilderness Act)

RCRA	Resource Conservation and Recovery Act
RD	Remedial Design (CERCLA)
RECLAIM	Regional Clean Air Incentives Market
RI/FS	Remedial Investing/Feasibility Study (CERCLA)
ROD	Record of Decision
RPAR	Rebuttable Presumption Against Registration (ToSCA)
RR	Relative Risk
RRA	Resource Recovery Act
RRRSC	Relative Risk Reduction Strategies Committee
SAE	Society of Automotive Engineers
SARA	Superfund Amendment and Reauthorization Act
SAV	Submerged Aquatic Vegetation
SCLDF	Sierra Club Legal Defense Fund, now Earth Justice
SCS	U.S. Soil Conservation Service (DoA)
SDWA	Safe Drinking Water Act
SEIS	Supplementary Environmental Impact Statement (NEPA)
SEP	Supplemental Environmental Project
SESCA	Michigan Soil Erosion and Sediment Control Act
SFAS-5	A Standard of Financial Accounting, incorporating environmental liabilities
SIC	Standard Industrial Classification
SIP	State Implementation Plan (CAA)
SIR	Supplemental Information Report (NEPA)
SIU	Significant Industrial Users (CWA)
SLAPP	Strategic Lawsuits Against Public Policy
SMCRA	Surface Mining Control and Reclamation Act
SMOA	Superfund Memorandum of Agreement
SMP	Supplemental Mitigation Projects (CWA)
SO^2	Sulfur Dioxide
SPCC	Spill Prevention, Control, and Countermeasure (CERCLA)

SPDES	State Pollutant Discharge Elimination System (CWA)
SPP	Stormwater Prevention Plans (CWA)
SRF	State Revolving Loan Funds (CWA)
Superfund	CERCLA
SWDA	Solid Waste Disposal Act
SWRCB	State Water Resources Control Board, a division of a state DEQ (California)
TCE	Trichloroethylene
TCLP	Toxicity Characteristic Leaching Procedure
TCMs	Transportation Control Measures (CAA)
TCP	Trichlorophenol
TDRs	Transferable Development Rights
TIP	Transportation Improvement Plan (ISTEA)
TOC	Total Organic Carbon
ToSCA	Toxic Substance Control Act
TRE	Toxicity Reduction Evaluation (CWA)
TRI	Toxics Release Inventory
TRO	Temporary Restraining Order
TSCA	ToSCA
TSD	Treatment, Storage, and Disposal (CERCLA)
TSS	Total Suspended Solids; Submerged aquatic vegetation (SAV)
TTP	Trial Type Process (APA)
TVA	Tennessee Valley Authority
U.S.S.G.	U.S. Sentencing Guidelines
UAA	Use Attainability Analysis (CWA)
UCATA	Uniform Contribution Among Tortfeasors Act
UCFA	Uniform Comparative Fault Act
UIC	Underground Injection Control
UNCED	United Nations Conference on Environment and Development
UNCLOS	United Nations Law of the Sea (treaties)
UNEP	United Nations Environment Programme

USDA	U.S. Department of Agriculture
USFS	U.S. Forest Service (DoA), or United States Forest Service (*see* FS)
USGAO	United States General Accounting Office (*see* GAO)
UST	Underground Storage Tank
VOC	Volatile Organic Compounds
WET	Whole Effluent Testing (CWA)
WIPP	Waste Isolation Pilot Project
WLA	Wasteload Allocation
WQBEL	Water Quality Based Effluent Standards (CWA)
WQS	Water Quality Standards (CWA)
WRC	Water Resources Commission (Michigan)
WRP	Wetlands Reserve Program (CWA)
WSRA	Federal Wild and Scenic Rivers Act
WTO	World Trade Organization
ZEV	Zero Emission Vehicles (automobiles)
ZID	Zones of Initial Dilution

Appendix C

SAMPLE RETENTION AGREEMENT

[Date]

[Name]
[Address]

Re: Attorney–Client Fee Contract

Dear _____:

This document ("agreement") is the written fee contract that [Insert legal requirement, if applicable]. [Name of Law Firm] ("we" or "us") will provide services to _____ ("_____" or "you") on the terms set forth below.

1. CONDITIONS. This agreement will not take effect, and we will have no obligation to provide legal services, until you return a signed copy of this agreement [and pay the initial deposit called for under Paragraph __].

2. SCOPE OF SERVICES. You are hiring us as your attorneys, to represent or advise you in connection with _____. We will provide those legal services reasonably required and requested to represent and advise you on the described matter, and on other related matters that you subsequently request and we agree to undertake on your behalf. We will take reasonable steps to keep you informed of progress and to respond to your inquiries. We will communicate to [Client] through [Name], unless we are instructed otherwise. [(Attorney Name) will be the principal attorney in charge of your matter, and (Attorney Name(s)) will assist. From time to time other attorneys in this firm, and if approved by you in advance, attorneys from other firms, will support our efforts.] A more detailed description of the work we have been retained to undertake is contained in the attached

"Scope of Work." Unless you and we make a different agreement in writing, this agreement will govern all future services we may perform for you.

3. CLIENT'S DUTIES. You agree to cooperate with us and be reasonably available to confer with us upon request, to keep us informed of developments, and to disclose to us all facts and circumstances of which you are aware that may bear upon our handling of the matter. You agree to provide us with such documents and information as you may possess relating to the matter, to abide by this agreement, to pay our bills on time, and to keep us advised of your address, telephone number, and whereabouts.

4. COORDINATION. We will coordinate the rendition of our services with the requirements of the corporation's other counsel, if you so request. We will take direction from you, as [Corporate Position and Title], unless we are instructed otherwise by the corporation. We will be entitled to assume that your directions are the corporation's instructions.

5. DEPOSIT OF ADVANCE PAYMENT. You agree to pay us an initial [Retainer?] deposit of [$3,000 normally] as an advance against fees. The deposit is not a retainer, but instead will be held in a trust account. You authorize us to use that fund to pay the fees and other charges you incur. Our billings, which are calculated and submitted on a monthly basis, will be made against this advance, which we expect to be kept current, i.e., replenished as the monthly billings are made against it. The monthly billings will be sent directly to you, and we will expect the advance to be replenished within thirty (30) days of the date of the billing.

6. LEGAL FEES AND BILLING PRACTICES. You agree to pay by the hour at our prevailing rates for time spent on your matter by our legal personnel. We record our time, and will bill you, to the nearest one-tenth hour. Our current hourly rates for legal personnel (and other billing rates) are set forth on the attached Rate Schedule. These rates are

reviewed and adjusted periodically, but not more frequently than annually. We will send you a proposed revision to our rates before effectuating any adjustment. The revised schedule of rates will apply after each adjustment.

We will charge you for the time we spend on telephone calls relating to your matter, including calls with you, [your general, special, or cooperating counsel,] opposing counsel, court personnel, experts, consultants, and witnesses. The legal personnel assigned to your matter will confer among themselves about the substantive legal, tactical, and strategic issues pertaining to the matter, and with consultants and other persons who may have information regarding your matter, as required. When they do confer, each of the legal personnel will charge for the time expended. Likewise, if more than one of our legal personnel attends a meeting, court hearing, or other proceeding, each will charge for the time spent. We will charge for waiting time in court and elsewhere and for travel time, both local and out of town.

7. COSTS AND OTHER CHARGES. We will incur various costs and expenses in performing legal services under this agreement. The cost of normal photocopying, long distance telephone calls, postage, and other small miscellaneous expenses as to which individual itemization is impractical are covered and included within our billing rates. All other costs, such as expert consultant and investigation fees, airfare, air charter, mileage at the IRS reimbursement rate, lodging, meals, deposition transcripts, document databasing if requested by you, filing fees, computerized legal research, unusual photocopying, and staff overtime, if and to the extent required, are billed directly on a pass-through basis as a cost advanced by us. We generally do not pass through our secretarial overtime costs unless the overtime is required due to unanticipated time constraints or other urgencies that arise in the matter. In case of significant costs, such as, for example, fees to employ consultants, we will ask that you deposit an estimate of those costs with us.

8. BILLING STATEMENTS. Our billings are calculated and submitted on a monthly basis. The billings are accompanied by a computer-generated statement setting forth a description of the services performed, the date of the work, the amount of time spent, and the identity of the person performing the work. Each statement will be due and payable upon presentation, and overdue thirty (30) days after the date of billing. Your account is considered current when payment is made within thirty (30) days of the billing date. [Late payments may require us to add an interest charge, which will be two percent (2%) above the reference rate of [insert name of bank].] We will send the original monthly statement to you at the address above, unless you instruct us otherwise.

If your account becomes delinquent, we have established collection procedures that may include stopping all legal services of a non-emergency nature. Contrary to our anticipation, if that situation should arise and exist for a period of sixty (60) days, we will ask you for, and you agree to execute, a stipulation allowing us to withdraw as your counsel of record.

9. LIEN. You hereby grant us a lien on claims or causes of action that are the subject of our representation under this agreement. Our lien will be for any sums owing to us at the conclusion of our services. The lien will attach to any recovery you may obtain, whether by arbitration award, judgment, settlement, or otherwise.

10. DISCHARGE AND WITHDRAWAL. You may discharge us at any time, and without cause, by giving us written notice of termination. We may withdraw with your advance written consent, or at any time after having given you written notice and a reasonable period within which to retain the services of other counsel.

When our services conclude, all unpaid charges will become due and payable immediately. After our services conclude, we will, on your request, deliver your file to you, along with any funds or property of yours in our possession.

11. DISCLAIMER OF GUARANTEE. Nothing in this agreement and nothing in our statements to you will be construed as a promise or guarantee about the outcome of your matter. We make no such promises or guarantees. Our comments about the outcome of your matter are expressions of opinion only.

12. COMMUNICATIONS. We encourage you to contact us at any time you have any question whatsoever concerning our representation of you.

13. OTHER REPRESENTATION. You acknowledge that [Name of Law Firm] has disclosed that they represent _____. [Name of Law Firm] represents that it does not have conflicts of interest with respect to services and matters that are specifically identified within the scope of this agreement. You agree that [Name of Law Firm]'s representation of _____ on the matters specifically described in this agreement shall not affect [Name of Law Firm]'s ability to represent _____. In the event that a future potential conflict arises between [Name of Law Firm]'s representation of _____, and you, [Name of Law Firm] and you will discuss the potential need to withdraw from or terminate this agreement, and/or a waiver of any such potential conflict. You agree that in the event of any such withdrawal or termination, you waive any conflict regarding [Name of Law Firm]'s continued representation of _____, and you shall not object to [Name of Law Firm]'s continued representation of _____. You agree that [Name of Law Firm]'s representation of you on this matter shall not affect [Name of Law Firm]'s ability to represent _____ on any unrelated matter, and you expressly waive any potential conflict of interest related thereto.

14. EFFECTIVE DATE. This agreement will take effect when you have performed the conditions stated in Paragraph 1, but its effective date will be retroactive to the date we first per-

formed services. The date at the beginning of this agreement is for reference only. Even if this agreement does not take effect, you will be obligated to pay us the reasonable value of any services we may have performed for you.

[Name of Law Firm]

By _____

Encl. (Schedule of Rates)

I/We have read and understood the foregoing terms and those set forth on the attached Rate Schedule and agree to them, as of the date [Name of Law Firm] first provided services. If more than one party signs below, we each agree to be liable, jointly and severally, for all obligations under this agreement.

[CLIENT]

By _____

[Name]

[Address]

_____

_____

_____

ATTACH CURRENT SCHEDULE OF RATES

Appendix D

SAMPLE SCOPE OF WORK OUTLINE

Scope of Work—Legal Fees

The scope of work under the Attorney–Client Fee Contract and related estimated fees are as follows:

First, we would provide a general overview of [area of law involved] that would be utilized as a primer for the lay audience, many of whom reside in the eastern portion of the United States.

Second, we would add to this base an analysis of [in this case a specific subset of information of interest to the client].

Third, we would include in our opinion a [a general description of information needed by the client]. In this regard we will respond to the following questions:

- [The client provided or had worked with me to pose six "bullets" that covered a range of issues.]

The first task is fairly straightforward. The second and third tasks might need further development as part of the analyses. We intend to provide you with a complete draft of the document for our discussion, prior to putting it into its final form and, assuming prompt approval, could have this draft completed by [date]. I estimate that fees for this work would be about [dollar estimate].

I would, of course, also be available to make presentations, discussing the opinion and responding to questions, if this was desired. I have not estimated the costs associated with these presentations.

This type of scope of work is fairly tight. I have drafted others over the years that have been much broader in their coverage. These broader documents have broken down tasks in sequence and have placed them on timelines. In this regard, each task has been assigned an estimate of fees and costs, and built into the timelines has been time to meet with the client, review our progress, and discuss current estimates of fees and costs.

Appendix E

SAMPLE BROCHURE FORMAT

[FIRM LETTERHEAD]
[DATE]

The first paragraph should be a general description of the firm. For example:

[NAME OF FIRM] brings a unique combination of experience to the fields of water, power, natural resources, public agency and public employment, public land, toxics and hazardous waste, environmental, zoning, planning, and land development law, and the defense of persons and corporations charged with environmental crimes. Firm attorneys are skilled in all phases of litigation before state and federal courts and administrative tribunals, and work closely together to provide their private and public agency clients with the benefit of their experience.

This opening paragraph is followed by a brief biography of each attorney. For example, my latest brief biography reads as follows:

Stuart L. Somach: Mr. Somach's background includes the U.S. Department of the Interior and the U.S. Department of Justice. In private practice since 1984, his practice concentrates on water rights, water quality, federal reclamation law, toxics, natural resources, and environmental law, all phases of litigation before federal and state courts, and negotiating federal legislative issues. He is a University of the Pacific, McGeorge School of Law Adjunct Professor of Law, having taught natural resources law, water quality, and toxics law. Mr. Somach has authored numerous articles in the area of natural resources and environmental law and speaks routinely on topics within his legal specialty. He is admitted to the State Bar of California and the District of Columbia Bar. He is a past Chairman of the American Bar Association's Committee on Water Resources Law.

Appendix F

SAMPLE ONE-PAGE RÉSUMÉ

I will often include, along with the "short form" of firm information included as part of the sample firm brochure, a short or long version of my and/or other attorneys' résumé of background and experience. The one-page résumé is formatted as follows:

[NAME OF ATTORNEY]

[FIRM LETTERHEAD]

Current Position

[Title; how long with firm.]

Areas of Practice Emphasis

[Personalize to the attorney and to the work involved.]

Prior Position

[Describe all relevant and helpful prior work.]

Bar Admissions

[Include all state bar information as well as courts in which the attorney is admitted to practice.]

Legal Education

Undergraduate Education

I also often use a longer version of the above which includes information on (1) academic positions I have held; (2) professional affiliations; (3) publications; and (4) presentations. I have added to this résumé over time so that it provides a comprehensive view of my experience and background.

Appendix G

SAMPLE PROPOSAL LETTER

Date]

[Name]
[Address]

Re: Proposal for Legal Services

Dear _____:

I enjoyed talking with you earlier this week and hope you found the article I provided to you of some interest. As I indicated to you when we spoke, in light of the personalities involved, the problem you outlined to me is not surprising. It is also of some significance given the public policy ramifications if you are not allowed to proceed as you have proposed. As I also indicated to you, I am very familiar with the general factual situation that is presented along with the legal and policy issues that are involved. I am very comfortable in stating that you would be hard pressed to find another firm better situated to assist you than [Name of Law Firm].

Firm Background and Experience

[Name of Law Firm] is a firm of [number] attorneys, all of whom specialize in the area of environmental law [add specifics here with respect to the nature of the firm's practice]. There are few firms within [State], or elsewhere, with as many attorneys devoted to these limited and specialized areas of law. [Insert more specific details about the firm and its practice.] In the area of [area of specialty] there is simply no situation, transactional or litigation related, that we cannot handle. I have enclosed for your review and information general materials about the firm and its attorneys.

In proceeding with the work that you outlined to me, it seems to me that the first step might be an attempt to negotiate some type of reasonable resolution with the _____.
I have had years of experience dealing with these types of matters,

and believe I could be of some assistance to you in attempting to avoid litigation.

In the event that a reasonable resolution cannot be negotiated, we can, of course, represent you in litigation. The attorneys within [Name of Law Firm] all have litigation experience. Some of that experience is quite extensive. For example, [insert detailed examples].

Over the years [Name of Law Firm] has been involved in major [insert specific areas of focus]. This litigation has been tried in both state and federal courts and has ranged from trial to appellate work. In addition, [Name of Law Firm] attorneys have tried these types of cases in [list other jurisdictions or states]. Indeed, we currently and actively represent parties in litigation in [list examples]. Again, because of our size and focus, we are able to marshal an amazing array of resources, as needed, in any particular litigation situation.

Two matters we have dealt with that are of particular relevance to the situation with which you are faced may be of interest. [Insert specific examples, if appropriate.]

Attorney Assignments

As noted above, I would lead our firm's work effort. I would also involve _____ and _____. [Provide details of these attorneys' backgrounds.] I have enclosed more detailed resumes of their background and experience for your information and review.

Representative Clients and Areas of Practice

The following list is representative of the public entity clients, private nonprofit association clients, and private sector clients we represent on issues and litigation involving a wide variety of water law and public agency matters:
1. [public entity clients]
2. [private sector and nonprofit association clients]

References

[Insert at least three or four references.]

Rates

A schedule of rates is enclosed. We record our time in tenths of an hour, multiply our time by our standard hourly rates, and bill monthly. We include in our statements the actual costs of express package services, substantial photocopying costs, mileage, airfare or aircraft rental, meals and lodging, and other expenses related to the provision of our services. We periodically examine our schedule and occasionally raise our rates.

In closing, I would like to reiterate [Name of Law Firm]'s capacity to provide experienced legal counsel to the [insert name of prospective client]. We are available to meet with you and/or your Board at your convenience to further discuss this matter. In the meantime, please do not hesitate to contact me if you have any questions or need additional information.

Very truly yours,

_____

Attorney

Encl.

Appendix H

SELECTED ABA PUBLICATIONS

Brownfields and Real Estate Law

ABA Section of Natural Resources, Energy, and Environmental Law and George Washington University Law School. *The Environmental Lawyer.*

Todd S. Davis and Kevin D. Margolis, Editors. *Brownfields A Comprehensive Guide to Redeveloping Contaminated Property.* 1997.

Elizabeth Glass Geltman. *Prospective Purchaser Agreements Reducing the Liability Risks of Contaminated Property.* 1997.

Thomas E. Root. *Railroad Land Grants.* 1987.

James B. Witkin, Editor. *Environmental Aspects of Real Estate Transactions.* 1995.

Air Quality/Clean Air

Charles H. Knauss, Shannon S. Broome, and Michael E. Ward. *The Clean Air Act Operating Permit Program: A Handbook for Counsel, Environmental Managers, and Plant Managers.* 1993.

Robert J. Martineau, Jr., and David P. Novello, Editors. *The Clean Air Act Handbook.* 1997.

Regulatory Compliance

Richard P. Fahey. *Underground Storage Tanks: A Primer on the Federal Regulatory Program,* Second Edition. 1995.

Theodore L. Garrett, Editor. *The RCRA Practice Manual.* 1994.

Theodore L. Garrett and Joshua D. Sarnoff, Editors. *RCRA Policy Documents: Finding Your Way through the Maze of EPA Guidance on Solid and Hazardous Waste.* 1993.

Elizabeth Glass Geltman. *A Complete Guide to Environmental Audits.* 1997.

James M. Kuszaj. *The EPCRA Compliance Manual: Interpreting and Implementing the Emergency Planning and Community Right-to-Know Act of 1986.* 1997.

Owen L. Schmidt. *Checklists for Preparing National Environmental Policy Act Documents.* 1998.

Carole Stern, John A. McKinney, Jr., and David B. Graham, Editors. *CERCLA Enforcement: A Practitioner's Compendium of Essential EPA Guidance and Policy Documents.* 1996.

Kristina M. Woods. *Identification of RCRA-Related Substances: How to Determine if Your Company is Handling a Hazardous Waste and Possible Ways to Soften the Blow.* 1989.

Water Law

Kathleen Marion Carr and James D. Crammond, Editors. *Water Law: Trends, Policies and Practice.* 1995.

Parthenia B. Evans, Editor. *The Clean Water Act Handbook.* 1994.

Practice Issues

Jay G. Foonberg. *How to Start and Build a Law Practice,* Fourth Edition. 1999.

Nancy Byerly Jones. *Easy Self-Audits for the Busy Law Office.* 1999.

R. Steven Morton, Editor. *What to Do When the Environmental Client Calls,* Second Edition. 1994.

Technology/Internet

Andrew Z. Adkins III. *Computerized Case Management Systems: Choosing and Implementing the Right Software for You.* 1998.

Joshua D. Blackman and David Jank. *The Internet Fact Finder for Lawyers: How to Find Anything on the Net.* 1998.

Kenneth E. Johnson. *The Lawyer's Quick Guide to E-mail.* 1998.

Jerry Lawson. *The Complete Internet Handbook for Lawyers.* 1999.

Gregory A. Siskind and Timothy Moses. *The Lawyer's Guide to Marketing on the Internet.* 1996.

Reference Manuals

Richard J. Fink, Editor. *The Natural Resources Law Manual.* 1995.

Gary A. Munneke and Anthony E. Davis. *The Essential Formbook: Comprehensive Management Tools for Lawyers.* 1999.

Index